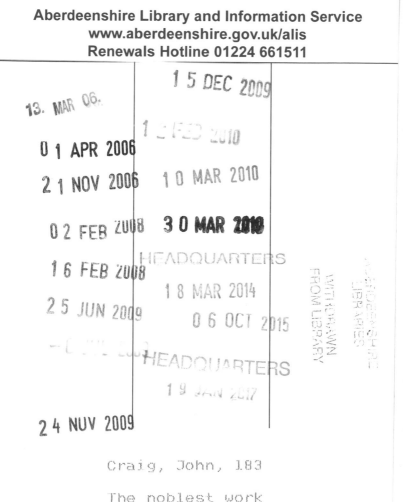

THE NOBLEST WORK OF GOD.

THE NOBLEST
WORK OF GOD

Episodes of My Life:
The story of John Craig,
Shipbuilding Entrepreneur, Toledo, Ohio

and

Memoirs of James Lough,
Master Mariner, Eyemouth,
formerly of Toledo, Ohio

As recorded by both in 1928 and 1929

Compiled and edited by Peter Aitchison

Birlinn

This edition first published in Great Britain
in 2005 by Birlinn Ltd
West Newington House
10 Newington Road
Edinburgh
EH9 1QS
www.birlinn.co.uk

General Introduction and Editorial Commentary
Copyright © Peter Aitchison 2005

ISBN 1 84158 392 8

British Library Cataloguing-in-Publication Data
A catalogue record is available on request

Typeset by Hewer Text Ltd, Edinburgh
Printed by Antony Rowe Ltd, Chippenham, Wiltshire

Dedicated in loving memory of
Jasmin Lough Dale Waddell Aitchison
Great grand-daughter of James Lough,
Kinswoman of John Craig and
Mother of Peter Aitchison

CONTENTS

ILLUSTRATIONS

ACKNOWLEDGEMENTS

This book started as a loose collection of stories handed down in an oral tradition through my grandmother Margaret Purves Lough Dale Waddell. They would have remained as family myths and legends had it not been for the historical detective work that was carried out by Patricia Smethurst of Maine, USA and which led to the discovery of the two remarkable documents which follow. Pat also helped in the drafting of the introduction – helpfully, and also cheerfully, pointing out errors and omissions. Along with her husband, Kevan, Pat spent two days driving from Maine in order to meet me in Toledo in the spring of 2004.

The historical context has been made much easier because of the advice of a number of people who subsequently became involved in the search for the real James Lough and John Craig. The archivist at Bowling Green State University provided much more than research material. Bob Graham answered my frequent inquiries with good humour and offered a wealth of important material. Bob also copied some of the images which are contained in the following pages. Without his assistance and the generous decision of Bowling Green University to allow the use of both the Craig and Lough memoirs which they hold, this book could never have been printed. I am very much in their debt.

I worked with my friend and colleague Andrew Cassell on a special documentary for BBC Radio Scotland which is based on *The Noblest Work of God*. As ever Andy probed aspects of the story and helped clarify in my mind the most salient and important points. I would expect little else from a journalist of the calibre and quality of Andrew Cassell. Together we visited Toledo and then Long Beach, California. In Ohio we were made welcome and assisted by Michael Lora of Toledo-Lucas County Public Library, Harry Archer of the West Lake Erie Historical Society and by local historian Ken Dickson. Ken provided a bulky folder stuffed full of detailed information. Jim Lynch, the assistant manager at what is now the Toledo Ship Repair Company, allowed us free access to the site and brought the story of the yard up to date. Happily ships are again being built on the side of the Maumee River.

I am indebted to Julie Steele of the Collingwood United Methodist Church in Toledo who helped trace another of my distant cousins. Scott Crim is the great-great-grandson of Willie Purves: the only one of three family strands which left Scotland in 1888 to settle permanently in Toledo.

My thanks are also due in very large measure to the people I met when I visited California. Jim and Bob Craig, the great-grandsons of John Craig, and Jim's wife Patricia not only opened up their family archives, but gave me the kind of welcome that defies description. I only hope that I can repay some of their kindness in future years when they, perhaps along with Scott Crim and Patricia Smethurst, visit the 'old country'.

I should also like to acknowledge the help of Mrs Kate Bolton, the present owner of James Lough's home in Eyemouth, who welcomed me into the house and gave me access to the original title deeds.

Even given all of the above help this book would still not have been possible but for the support and encouragement of my wife Gillian and our children David, Jennifer and Jack. Gillian worked tirelessly on transcribing both the scrawled Lough manuscript and the biography of John Craig. She also asked the right questions and sometimes the most pertinent and searching questions. This book is as much hers as it is mine.

But it would never have been written at all but for the stories handed down by the matriarch, Peggy Purves Lough Dale Waddell. Every conversation with that remarkable old lady has brought further detailed and intricate and moving accounts of the lives and adventures of ordinary people she has known or been told of: of James Lough, Maggie Purves and John Craig.

A final word must go to my late mother Jasmin Lough Dale Waddell Aitchison. She died before this book had even been started. It is dedicated in most humble and loving terms to her memory.

GENEALOGICAL DIAGRAM

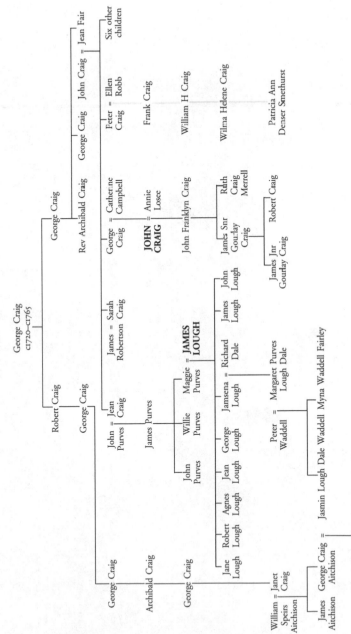

George Craig
c1720–c1765

Robert Craig

George Craig

George Craig

George Craig

Archibald Craig

George Craig

John = Jean Craig
Purves

James Purves

John
Purves

Willie
Purves

Maggie = JAMES
Purves   LOUGH

Jane   Robert   Agnes   Jean   George   Jamsena = Richard   James   John
Lough   Lough   Lough   Lough Lough   Lough   Dale   Lough   Lough

Margaret Purves
Lough Dale

Peter =
Waddell

Jasmin Lough Dale Waddell Myrna Waddell Fairley

William = Janet
Speirs   Craig
Aitchison

James   George Craig
Aitchison Aitchison

PETER WADDELL AITCHISON

Rev Archibald Craig

George = Catherine
Craig   Campbell

JOHN = Annie
CRAIG   Losee

John Franklyn Craig

James Snr   Ruth
Gourlay   Craig
Craig   Merrell

James Jnr   Robert Craig
Gourlay Craig

George Craig

Peter = Ellen
Craig   Robb

Frank Craig

William H Craig

Wilma Helene Craig

Patricia Ann
Denser Smerhurst

John Craig = Jean Fair

Six other
children

GENERAL INTRODUCTION

This is the story of John Craig and James Lough: two remarkable, yet ordinary men who lived through years of breathtaking change and breakneck development. Together their lives extend from the fourth decade of the nineteenth century to the fifth of the twentieth century. They link the dying days of the Wild West in the United States to the sweat and toil of Scotland's sail fishermen; the horror yet hope of the American Civil War to the freezing waters of the North Sea in the equally ambiguous Great War; and above all else they link the dignity and intimacy of the ordinary man and his family wherever life and fate might take them.

Each tells his own story in memoirs which were either written down or dictated in 1928 and 1929. As such the language is often as raw as the emotion that pours across the pages. Humour is there too, along with immense sorrow as the two branches of the same family struggled to get ahead. One would achieve the American dream of wealth, prestige and power – with business interests across two states, political influence which almost led to a Presidential nomination in 1908 and an eventual home in Country Club Drive, Long Beach, California. The other strand of the family was equally ambitious. But after spending time in America the decision was taken to return home to Scotland. While the opportunities were less pronounced, they were nonetheless grasped with the same verve and energy.

It has been estimated that around two million Scots went overseas during the course of the nineteenth century, but that around a third of these came back – scunnered, disillusioned, unable to seize the moment or just plain homesick. The story of these two Berwickshire families – the Craigs of Coldingham and the Loughs of Eyemouth – gives flesh to that statistic and offers a telling perspective on the life of the common man.

Neither biography was written with the general reader in mind. The first, *Episodes of My Life* by John Craig, came out in a private print run of just one hundred bound copies in the United States in 1928. The existence of the second, which was untitled but which I have chosen to call *The Noblest Work of God*, was unknown even to those closest to James Lough when he penned it in Eyemouth in the following year. It only came to light when Patricia Smethurst, a distant American cousin, formerly of California but now living in Maine, contacted me after reading my book on the Eyemouth Fishing Disaster. She knew of the existence of the memoir which had been sent to the United States shortly after it was completed and which had lain forgotten for close on eighty years.

Yet many of the stories contained within both of these unique and important historical documents were familiar to me. My mother's middle name was Lough, my father's is Craig. My grandmother, Margaret Purves Lough Dale Waddell, known to all as Peggy Dale, is the granddaughter of James Lough. She has kept alive an oral tradition which sometimes offers intricate detail and other times gives only back-handed whispers of things that might have happened. Peggy Dale also retains a family heirloom: a sheet of linen, woven in the eighteenth century by the common ancestor of all of these family strands, George Craig, weaver of Coldingham. Born c.1720, died c.1765.

In his youth George had watched as the Jacobite host won the first major engagement of the 1745 rising at Prestonpans in East Lothian. It is probable that the Craigs still worked on the land at this time, but that link with the soil was broken within a decade or so of the crushing of the Jacobite rebellion. While history has remembered the destruction of the clan system and the highland clearances that followed the shattering of the '45, the wholesale changes that were also reaped in the lowlands, if they are remembered at all, are referred to in more benign terms as 'agricultural improvement'. The language we use today would have made no difference to the pain which lowland 'cottars' must have felt when they lost their grip on their traditional lands. By choice or by force, the Craigs were villagers and not country folk by the middle of the eighteenth century.

George had several children and the family continued to work as outsourced weavers. But that cottage industry came under increasing pressure from the new industrial mills of the towns and cities. By the opening decade of the nineteenth century other options had to be pursued. One branch of the Craigs flitted three miles south from Coldingham where old George's grandson, also called George, founded a dynasty of fishermen in the fast-growing coastal centre of Eyemouth.

Another grandson, Archibald Craig, showed what could be achieved by any lad-o-pairts in Scotland by enrolling at Edinburgh University and later becoming both a renowned Greek scholar and a distinguished minister in the Kirk. Archie's elder brother John clung on to spinning linen – but he must have battled against the new array of machines that could produce infinitely more cloth at a fraction of the price of the former artisans of labour.

In 1827 and at the age of just eighteen John Craig's son, who to confuse matters was also called George, joined the army of migrants at Greenock quay. He was set for Quebec, a hazardous journey which would take several weeks in a cramped and stinking emigrant ship. George went alone but he took with him the hopes of his family, having promised to send back for the rest of the clan as soon as he had saved enough money. This he did, and with the exception of two married sisters, Jean and Sarah (and possibly a third called Ellen), one whole side of the Craig line left Scotland for good in the early 1830s.

In 1838 the first American member of the family was born with the arrival of George's first child. John Craig would live the American dream and come to mix with the major players in stateside politics and industry like Abraham Lincoln, Horace Greeley, Andrew Carnegie and others. John Craig became a successful entrepreneur, a man of great wealth and influence. Yet throughout it all he maintained contact with the Old Country and with his Scottish relatives, especially Willie, John and Maggie Purves. He also struck up a tremendous and lasting friendship with Maggie's husband, James Lough.

Lough and Craig were born thousands of miles apart and might never have met or even known of each other's existence had the bonds that linked migrants and their kin back home not been as strong in the south of Scotland as has long been accepted was the norm for those from the north and west. But these links were real and did endure.

They drew John Craig to visit his family's old home in Berwickshire on at least three occasions and in the summer of 1888 it prompted conversations, on the rain-pelted quayside of Eyemouth, of opportunity for anyone with drive and determination. Craig, by then a shipbuilder on the Great Lakes, argued American protectionism against British free trade. The words may have sailed over the heads of men more used to pricing herring barrels and haddock lines, but they imbibed like a Saturday night drunk the wonders of America. Eyemouth was suffering like it had never suffered before. In the Great Disaster of Friday October 14th 1881, one in three of the town's men had drowned in a fearful hurricane which tore the fleet apart and destroyed the community's future. Many of the 129 men who were lost were dragged to the deep within a stone's throw of the very pier that Craig was then holding court upon. Murdered by the ocean within full view of their wives, mothers and bairns. Amongst the dead was John Craig's own cousin, James Purves – the father of Willie, John and Maggie Purves.

Eyemouth, which had been a thrusting, ambitious and defiant little place, imploded in the wake of Black Friday. The fishermen, once renowned for their skill and bravery, now instinctively took to creeping along the inshore waters, petrified of the fate that would befall them should they strike out further. The value of quayside catches went into freefall – from close on £60,000 in the year of the Disaster to a little over £10,000 when John Craig's carriage thrashed over the moor of Coldingham just seven years later. Trade would continue spiralling downwards well into the twentieth century.

Families were pushed to the edge of starvation, and where before there was money aplenty for weekend sprees in the pub and expensive jaunts to Edinburgh, now all that the place seemed good for, to quote one commentator of the time, was 'thin kail, scant bread and soup kitchens'. The move away to the factories of the cities and the hop-off points at Greenock and Port Glasgow for a future in foreign parts had already begun to lure the desperate and the ambitious. So when John Craig spoke of America the audience had only one question. 'Would you give us a job if we came over there, Mr Craig?'

John Craig was on the brink of opening a new shipyard at Toledo, Ohio and his answer was 'Yes, if I could'. And that was enough to persuade two fishermen who had pushed themselves to the front of the throng. They warranted a better vantage point because they were second cousins of the celebrity American. John and William Purves' grandmother Jean had remained in Berwickshire along with her sister Sarah when the rest left Scotland for good in the early 1830s. Sarah by then was married to James Robertson, a Coldingham blacksmith. When he died at a young age she moved down the coast to Eyemouth to be close to her Craig cousins and to her sister Jean and her husband, fisherman John

Purves. John and Jean had several children, including a son, James who was born in 1831. While the Craigs of America would come to ply their trade as builders of boats, James Purves would win his bread by sailing them. He would become one of the stars in the fishing firmament. But his destiny was to be with death on Disaster Day. As skipper of the *Myrtle* he lashed himself to the tiller of the boat at the height of the Black Friday storm and died, with the other six men of his crew, when a single almighty wave overturned the flimsy craft and pulled it down to the ocean floor.

The loss of their father was an emotional blow; that of the family boat an economic tragedy. The Purves boys struggled to make ends meet. Whether through continuing bad luck or their reluctance to sail in all but the fairest weather, and then only for short trips, they could not find fish. With families to keep and debts to pay, John and Willie grasped the hand of John Craig. He offered the same prospect to their sister Maggie. But she was less certain. Though she lived in a tiny house in the centre of the cramped village, and was as poor as the rest of the fisherfolk, Maggie Purves loved Eyemouth. In any case when the offer was made her man was away at the Scarborough herring drave and Maggie would not commit without the word of James Lough. By the time Lough sailed through the roadsteads into the harbour, John Craig was well on his way back to America, doubting that his Eyemouth kin would ever take up his offer. He had left his address just in case, but heard no more from his Scottish cousins until they chapped at his door in Trenton, Michigan some weeks later.

James Lough had needed little persuading from his brothers-in-law, in spite of his wife's reticence. At the age of thirty-one, and with fishing providing little more than crusts, it was a golden opportunity for the family. James always wanted to better himself, to do well by Maggie, and to leave his children with more chances than he had been provided with. By 1888 James and Maggie already had four young bairns - Robert, George, Jean and Agnes – with another on the way. Their first-born, Jane, had died of measles at the age of three in 1885.

The three Eyemouth men took the high road for the Broomielaw and sailed from Glasgow in the late autumn of 1888. Six weeks after they left, Maggie Purves gave birth to another daughter – whom in the tradition of the town she named Jamesena, after her father who had perished on Black Friday. It was only by coincidence that it was also the name of her man, so far away from home, yet so much in her thoughts.

James Lough and John and Willie Purves had not considered wiring notice ahead when they left Eyemouth to cross an ocean for a world they had only the haziest notion about. They had been asked over by family, and that was good enough for them. The three men intended to work hard, save earnestly and then, if things were fine, to send back for their own folks to come over.

The trio arrived first in Quebec, before heading down the Great Lakes to Detroit and on, unannounced, to the Trenton home of John Craig. Stunned by their appearance, Craig offered this piece of advice: 'You boys have come here to get a few dollars, but you won't find them on the streets in America, you will find them in the trees'. While the Purves boys studied their shoes, James Lough instantly twigged the riddle. 'I see what you mean Mr Craig,' he said, 'You mean we will have to reach for them.'

Ambition and hard work would bring their rewards. That was the mantra of John Craig. But likewise it was the guiding principle of James Lough. It bonded their friendship.

That evening in Trenton, Craig told his wife Annie Losee that he doubted whether their Scottish visitors would remain long in the country. Perhaps he doubted their true ambition. But though she had only just met him, there was something about James Lough that prompted Mrs Craig to offer her view: 'I don't care very much about who goes home if James will stay here'.

John Craig had dragged himself up from his own perilous start in life. His father was the original migrant who had left Scotland in 1827. Arriving at the same Canadian port as James Lough would do sixty-one years later, and with the same sense of purpose, George Craig earned enough money to send first for his brother Peter, and then for his parents and his younger brother John and his sisters Sophie, Jeanette and Christiana. George's married sisters, Jean and Sarah, as mentioned, stayed in Scotland.

The Craigs stayed only a short time in Canada before heading down to New York. It was a move that would have tragic consequences. In 1834, a cholera epidemic swept through the densely packed city, claiming hundreds of victims. Amongst the dead were both of George Craig's parents, John Craig and Jean Fair. At the age of twenty-five and for the second time in his short life George Craig now had the responsibility of doing all he could for his family rather than for himself. As his son would later note, George knuckled down to the task and put personal ambition to one side for the greater good of his brothers and sisters.

The Craigs lived in an area known as the 'dry dock' in the Scottish quarter of the city, and George found work as a ship's sawyer. He married within that close knit society-within-a-society, taking Catherine Campbell, who hailed originally from Little Dunkeld in Perthshire, as his bride. Four children followed: three daughters – Jeanette and Jean and Catherine, who died in childhood – and one son, John, who was born on Christmas Eve 1838.

In 1852, and at the tragically young age of just forty-five, George's wife died. By then, however, Catherine Campbell had inculcated into her offspring a system of learning and of life that had its roots in the Scottish Presbyterian tradition. Unlike their cousins back in the rude fishing town of Eyemouth, these Craig children attended school every day, after which there were more lessons, followed by household chores and then bible reading – all under the watchful eye of their mother. For John Craig the learning would not stop, even after his beloved mother's death. Though he was only thirteen years old he continued to study and later enrolled as one of the youngest ever students in the New York Free Academy.

Education, and with it that 'system for life' which Catherine Campbell had hammered into him, remained with John Craig as the most important keys to unlocking the potential of an individual. Along with faith in God and trust in humanity, they pointed the path to prosperity.

The Craigs held together until 1849 when news seeped through of the California Gold Rush. It was agreed that either George or Peter, the two eldest boys, should draw lots to decide who would go west in search of a fortune. The other was to stay behind to look after the rest of the family. Peter won the draw and set out for California. Moving west at the same time was his sister Jeanette and her husband, a powerful New York medic called Dr Christopher Grattan. As agreed, George Craig stayed in the east apparently under a deal which held that should Peter strike it rich, then the money would be divided equally between them. That was certainly George's interpretation of the arrangement – especially when his brother arrived back in New York two years later a wealthy man. Peter's recollection was somewhat different and when he offered something less than a full share, George refused and a rift opened up within the Craig family.

Peter Craig opted to leave America and for a while he went back with his family to Scotland where he stayed in Eyemouth with his sister Sarah. Peter would also have come into contact with his other Scottish sister Jean Craig, her husband John Purves and their largely grown-up family, including their eldest son James. Eyemouth at that time was a booming fishing port and James Purves an ambitious and successful young fisherman. In September 1852, and just a matter of months after the visit of his uncle Peter, James married Jane Mack. Unusually for the age they had only three bairns – John, William and Maggie Purves.

Thirty-six years after Peter's 1852 sojourn in Berwickshire, his estranged brother George's son John Craig would make the same journey. He would entice his Purves cousins to follow the family trail to America.

Evidently Scotland was not to be a permanent home again for Peter Craig, his wife Ellen Robb and their three American-born children Alexander, John and Sarah. Perhaps it was never intended as anything more than an extended holiday or perhaps Peter's childhood memories of Scotland no longer matched the harsh reality of life in a fishing-toun. Peter Craig and his family were back in New York in time to sail once more for California on board the *Harriet Hoxie* which departed on March 23rd and arrived at the west coast on August 4th 1852.

The family settled in San Francisco where Peter and his eldest son Alexander Craig established an undertakers' business. Though Peter was successful and perfected a way of embalming corpses without the use of chemicals, the wealth which he had amassed in the Gold Rush did not last. In July 1881, frantic with worry over a business loss, Peter Craig committed suicide by hanging himself.

Back in New York, Peter's brother George had advanced from working as a ship's sawyer to a position as a coal and lumber trader. Indeed he had made enough money to make his own trip back to Scotland in 1853. During that short visit George met and became friends with another member of the family who had made great strides in life. Uncle Archibald Craig epitomised all that was possible within the Scottish Presbyterian system of education-for-all. His upbringing in the early years of the nineteenth century in the little village of Coldingham might have been spartan, but that did not prevent Archie from going on to become a Professor of Latin and Greek at the University of Edinburgh as well as a distinguished minister in the Church of Scotland. To the chagrin of the Yankee Craigs, who kept up a correspondence with

'Uncle Archie' until his death in 1876, their Scottish relative was an avowed supporter of the Confederacy during the Civil War. Archie took a particular interest in George's son – his own great-nephew – John Craig. That interest and obvious affection would later lead to a substantial bequest for John at a crucial time in his life.

George Craig's work, first as a sawyer and then as a trader, was centred on the teeming docks of New York City. These became boyhood playgrounds for young John, who stood transfixed as cargoes of goods and people poured out on to the wharfs. John Craig would later recall that one of his most cherished memories came in 1851, when he watched as the great yacht *America* sailed away to win the international trophy that thereafter took its name. Events like this propelled the boy into dreams of a life at sea, and he continually plagued his father with requests to be allowed at least to sail on a schooner owned by the family of one of his school friends.

But George Craig didn't push young John up a gangplank on an ocean-going lugger bound for who knew where and to return who knew when. Instead he arranged for the boy to start work, as he had done, as a junior ship's carpenter. This apprenticeship was the making of John Craig. It set him on the road to his eventual career as one of America's great shipbuilders.

Not content to simply learn on the job, and still 'learning' all he could whenever he had the chance, John engaged a colleague of his father to teach him ship design in the evenings. It was at that time, and while yet a youth, that he mentally laid down the dimensions of the *Amelia G. Ireland*, the first boat he would ever build for himself – though its actual construction came several years later. John Craig also took the opportunity to venture to Scotland for the first time, where, like his father and his uncle Peter, he stayed with his aunt and cousins and learned a different form of vessel construction at the Eyemouth boatbuilding yard.

John returned to an America that was hurtling towards Civil War. The drive by the southern states for secession developed an unstoppable momentum with the emergence of the exclusively northern Republican Party. Craig heard Lincoln speak at the Cooper Institute in New York in February 1860 and became a committed and lifelong Republican. He considered slavery abhorrent to God and wasteful of man's resources and he did his bit to help the north win the Civil War that broke out in the following year by helping complete twenty-three vessels for service.

These included the *USS Winona* which was built and delivered to the
government within sixty-three days of the contract being signed. The
ship was part of the Union fleet during the crucial engagement at
Vicksburg on the Mississippi.

The start of the Civil War marked a defining year for John Craig. In
that year, 1861, and at the age of twenty-two, John married his sweetheart
Annie Eliza Losee in New York. It was also at that time that Craig struck
out into business by entering a partnership with a shipbuilder called
Simonson. That business greatly benefited from the contracts issued by
the navy. As the war drew to a close, Craig, in spite of his own successes
and a personal fortune in excess of $2000, felt unfulfilled. 'By this time I
had been in business two years, [yet] I never had created anything by
myself and couldn't point to anything and say, "this is my handiwork".'
He entered into an agreement which took him down to Maryland where
he laid the hull and constructed the beams of his dream ship, the *Amelia
G. Ireland.*

Craig's account of his time 'Down South' and especially his comments
relating to Negroes make for some uncomfortable reading. The same
tone is apparent elsewhere in his memoirs and also when he describes
local people in Egypt and the Holy Land during a visit there in 1904. It
would have been remarkable had his invective been anything else.
Though an abolitionist, Craig did not subscribe to any fanciful notion
of racial equality. A war had been fought and hundreds of thousands of
white men had been killed to end slavery. That, for the time being,
seemed commitment enough to the black man.

The end of the war and the crushing of the rebellion brought joy to
the north, but it also brought economic depression. Craig could not find
a buyer for the *Amelia G. Ireland* and, not for the last time, his luck
turned sour. Personal tragedy compounded matters when, on his return
to New York, his infant son Peter died. Penniless and now with a broken
heart, John Craig was morose with grief. It took the strong will of his
wife, Annie Losee, to pull him back from the brink of despair. 'I resolved
to keep going if she could, and luck turned, for when one door closes
another one often opens up somehow and so it proved.'

John's two surviving sisters had married within the Scottish emigrant
community: Jeanette to businessman James Gourlay, originally from
Edinburgh, and Catherine to a tea trader called Alex Linn. Alex's Uncle
Robert, who had emigrated from Paisley in 1841, owned a shipyard on

the Great Lakes and through this network John Craig seized the chance of advancement. After working with Linn for a few months he took the huge step of a permanent move from the city of New York to the tiny settlement of Gibraltar, Michigan. It was hardly a fair swap and John felt for his wife who was forced to quit 'New York where all her family and friends lived, with all its comforts and privileges of concerts, church, lectures and going to a little town of not over 50 families – with about 200 army deserters, negro slaves who had run away from their masters. Think of it! What a desolate life she must have led in order that I could again have an opportunity to make good'.

Those hardships were endured and led to the founding of the Great Lakes shipbuilding firm of Linn and Craig. The company did well for the next few years and John Craig once more prospered. He built a house, and kept a happy home and a healthy bank balance.

But relations between John Craig and Robert Linn were rarely cordial. After a run on the banks precipitated the Great Panic of 1873, the business was in serious trouble and Craig again faced financial ruin. Rather than sit and wait for bankruptcy, however, he took one of the schooners the yard had completed and sailed it across the Great Lakes to Chicago in search of a buyer. The ploy paid off, but Craig had almost been brought to ruin for a second time. It was a chastening experience which he would never forget. 'This is one of the episodes of my life that caused me to think-think-think and I resolved and determined I would never be in debt again.'

It was at this point that news came through of the death back in Scotland of his great-uncle, Archie Craig. The sadness of the passing of the man was offset by the very welcome arrival of a substantial bequest of fifty pounds sterling. It helped John in the next step in his life's ambition. He resolved to end his partnership with Robert Linn. Craig was now approaching middle age, and apart from the deterioration of relations with his irascible Scottish associate, he wanted to strike out on his own. He was also acutely aware of how much his wife Annie detested Mrs Linn. In a letter to Robert, John wrote that they 'were so different from most other men and cannot talk without almost fighting . . . but when the women took up cudgels it was more than time for a change'.

In October 1878 the partnership of Linn and Craig was dissolved and John Craig set up his own shipyard in Gibraltar. Four years later he moved to Trenton but in 1888, after falling foul of labour laws in an attempt to bring foreign (Canadian) workers into his Michigan yard, John Craig turned south and started a new business in Toledo, Ohio. The city, founded in 1837, was an important trading crossroads which by the close of the nineteenth century was the third busiest railroad terminus in the United States after Chicago and St Louis. It offered a fine chance for advancement.

Before the Toledo yard was formally opened, John Craig spent several weeks touring shipyards in Britain to get ideas on what techniques and machinery would be necessary for the construction of steel-hulled vessels. He could see that the days of timber ships were drawing to an end and wanted to be in the vanguard of the exciting and potentially lucrative trade in ironclad hulls for both freight and passenger transport on the Great Lakes.

It was during this trip, in the summer of 1888, that Craig returned once more to his ancestral home of Berwickshire. There he stood on the pier at Eyemouth, beside the fishing boat yard he had laboured in thirty years before, and spoke of protectionism against free trade. It was then that he made a promise of work to his second cousins John and Willie Purves and by proxy, through their sister Maggie, to James Lough.

Lough, like Craig, had endured hard times as a youngster. But he too was a man of great principle and inner strength. And again like Craig, if those qualities ever wavered, they were set back on the plumbline by the love and guidance of his life-partner. With John Craig it was Annie Losee who shared the dreams and took away the pain of trouble. With James Lough it was Maggie Purves, whom he married in Eyemouth in 1879. The affection for Maggie shines through Lough's memoirs. He named the two ships he would come to own in her honour, and when Maggie died from illness in 1918 a part of James Lough left this earth with her.

James was always destined to be a fisherman. It was the calling of his father and his father's father. Unlike John Craig in New York and Archibald Craig in Coldingham, schooling did not provide an alternative route in Eyemouth. There were only two books in the Lough house. One of those was the bible and neither was well thumbed. As the eldest of seven children James had to gather mussels and limpets to bait his father's lines. This would take upwards of seven hours a day and it was work he would have done from the time he was about six years of age.

Classroom learning was an expensive waste of time for fishing folk. It wouldn't stir a pot or boil a kettle.

In the rough world of Eyemouth young James would have endured a 'brothering' before he reached his teenage years. This ritual involved some physical and a lot more psychological torture as boys were inducted into the world of men, of nets and lines, of strong whisky and profane language. They were then fostered out to crew up on the boats of other families where they would be hardened without any favours from their own kin.

It was not a world James Lough took to. He describes how his own salt tears mingled with the brackish sea water as he endured his first 'trip' at the age of twelve. Even when he fell overboard, still he was offered no help from the other men on the boat. They considered him worthless. 'But their words burnt into my memory and I determined to be a good fisherman and a good man in every respect.'

That sense of purpose is evident on almost every page of his memoir.

Lough put his all into the fishing, scrimped and saved and foreswore strong drink in order to amass enough money to buy his own boat, achieving, as he said, his first goal in life. He had already promised his sweetheart, Maggie Purves, that they would wed as soon as he had become a 'man like other men', and on 8th October 1879 'the best woman in this world became my wife'.

They set up home in a two-roomed garret in Chapel Street, and made a vow together that they would not waste what God and their own efforts had provided. In Eyemouth, where drink was the real religion, that meant the sacrilege of not keeping whisky in the house unless 'there was trouble', meaning a family bereavement or a drowning at sea.

It is impossible to exaggerate how hard it must have been to make that decision. Berwickshire fishermen traditionally divided their week's earnings at the home of a crewmember, usually the skipper, on a Saturday night. The money was doled out after each man had taken his fill from a huge cod which was smothered in a pound or two of butter and placed on a single plate in the centre of the table. To make the fish 'swim', beer and whisky were drunk to excess.

On that first Saturday night, as the six other members of Lough's crew dandered up the wooden staircase to their little home, Maggie Purves was beside herself with dread. But Lough stood firm and against the inevitable curses and hoots of derision refused point blank to allow liquor into his home. 'Now men, Maggie and I have made a vow that we will not break tonight, she will not bring strong drink here.'

In later years, and in spite of all that befell him, James remained solidly sober. The only time a drunk ever staggered through his home was when some of his own grandchildren managed to purloin a bottle of whisky which was kept for 'ill times' at the top of a wardrobe. John Windram and his cousin David Purves passed the bottle around before grabbing young Maggie Purves (namesake of her grandmother) and pouring the booze down her throat. The three of them then burst into the front room where their mothers and aunts were sipping tea with old James, all of whom had just returned home from a temperance meeting. The episode, which took place in the early 1920s, was witnessed by another of Lough's grandchildren, Peggy Dale, or Margaret Purves Lough Dale, as she had been christened. The incident caused uproar in the house and of course great glee to those in Eyemouth who did not share the Loughs' sober ideals.

At the end of their first year together, through thrift and hard work, Maggie had managed to 'put by' twenty pounds. 'We had made up our minds to better our circumstances,' Lough states, 'and we were prepared to deny ourselves to accomplish our aim.'

Almost two years to the day after their marriage the couple were touched, as all were in Eyemouth, by the catastrophe of the fishing disaster of 1881. James Lough, somehow, managed to make it into port on Black Friday, but the death toll of 129 local men included Maggie's own father, James Purves, as well as many uncles, cousins and second cousins. Maggie was pregnant, and amidst the sorrow and death a new life came into their troubled world: Jane Mack Purves was born on December 8th 1881. Her arrival was of no consolation to the widow after whom she was named. Maggie and James took Jane Mack into their home and nursed her and even softened their rule on drink in the house as the poor soul sought solace in a whisky bottle. But Jane Mack Purves, like so many other stricken women, stopped speaking, barely ate and eventually died of a broken heart.

There seemed no end to the ill luck that befell Maggie and James.

In August 1882 Lough's brother, Robert, was knocked overboard and drowned. James blamed himself for this because he had left Rob in charge of the family boat the *Border Rose* when he answered a plea to help crew up with his brothers-in-law, William and John Purves. But in so doing Lough left his own brother, who lacked experience, at the mercy of the North Sea. It is one of very few incidents in his memoirs that was unknown within the family tradition. James never spoke of the death of Robert Lough, yet the pain never left him. 'My brother, whom my hope for the future was built on,' he wrote more than forty years later, died because James had made the wrong choice of priorities. 'I have never forgiven myself and never will my foolish act in leaving our family boat.'

That death was followed in short order by the wasting-away of Jane Mack Purves in 1883 and then by the death of James's first daughter, three-year-old Jane Mack Lough. For two months the infant battled for life after contracting measles. Her death seemed to presage the end of the world for James Lough and Maggie Purves. 'We thought the sun would never shine any more in our home.'

Poor fishing, hard times, harsh winters followed. It must have seemed a never-ending spiral of despair. It is hardly surprising that when he returned from the Scarborough herring season in the autumn of 1888 to be told of the visit of John Craig, James seized the opportunity of a fresh start in America.

But to leave such a close-knit community was a major undertaking. And Maggie needed a lot of convincing. In a sense, yet in inverse proportions, it was like John Craig asking his wife Annie Losee to leave vast New York for the parochial settlement of Gibraltar. Each went from certainty to uncertainty; from the closeness of the familiar to something unknown and, in the case of America, totally foreign.

James Lough and John and Willie Purves may even have felt a sense of shame, a sense that they were abandoning Eyemouth at the very time that the town needed them. Around three hundred children had been left fatherless in the wake of Black Friday yet not a single bairn had been allowed to leave. All were looked after within the place because these young people were seen as the future. A call had even gone out around the coast for Eyemouth families who had left to come home and help rebuild the shattered community. Now here were three fine, healthy and ambitious young men opting to leave.

But each had substantial debts; James even had orders against him for non-payment of local government rates. If the jail didn't beckon, then maybe the poorhouse might. America promised so much more than home seemed able to offer.

The three Scots started work in the Toledo shipyard in the late spring of 1889. James in particular found it hard to knuckle down to obeying orders – as a skipper he had been his own master for ten years – but both he and his young brother-in-law Willie submitted to the discipline for the sake of their wives and bairns back home. Not so John Purves. He couldn't stick the work and within three months was off. John Craig's prediction that they would not all stay came true much quicker than probably even he had expected.

John Purves arrived back in Eyemouth a few weeks later and, as he had done on the outward journey to America, without any advance warning. 'Is that you, John', said his wife as he tripped into the kitchen. 'Aye it's me, whay do ye think it is?' 'Weel,' said his wife, 'I am ready to go to America.' 'Weel,' was John's reply, 'You can gang if ye like, but ah'm hame and I will bide at hame.' John never went back to America and his family live yet in Eyemouth.

That did not deter the wives and children of William Purves and James Lough. William's wife Christina had her son James in tow; Maggie Purves arrived in Canada en route to Ohio with her young children Robert, Agnes, Jean and the babe in arms Jamesena – born in December 1888 while her father was in America.

The party came in through Montreal and then on across the Lakes to Detroit where Maggie's great-uncle George Craig, the original migrant from Coldingham, was delighted to meet them. Also there was Maggie's brother Willie Purves who took the party on with him to Toledo. Willie was so anxious to show them the sights of their new home that he forgot about the rendezvous with James Lough who coursed up and down the town, almost going wild with worry. At the end of that day, convinced something had gone wrong, James trudged home in dejection – only to find Willie and Maggie and the bairns waiting for him in his own parlour.

Almost from that first moment Maggie made it clear that she was not for staying. Her home was Eyemouth, and while America might be fine to help them on their way, she told James that it could never be for good. Maggie Purves made a vow to remain for five years only. Like most, if not all, of that strong woman's promises, it was a promise kept . . . almost to the exact day.

The industrial waterfront of Toledo should have presented a familiar aspect to the Loughs. It was as rough as Eyemouth ever was, and with nine saloons and several bordellos across the way from the shipyard it surely gave Maggie and James an echo of home, especially when the bars shut at night and hordes of loud, rubber-limbed men poured out into the street.

Certainly the excesses of Toledo's pubs angered and frustrated James Lough who often helped the coloured night watchman protect the shipyards from drunks who tried to steal rowboats to get them across to the main part of the city on the opposite bank of the Maumee River. Lough paints a picture of lawlessness where only brute force and the authority of a firearm could keep the peace. In 1890 several hundred Hungarians arrived in Toledo to work both at the shipyard and at the nearby Malleable Iron Works. These 'Balkan men', as Lough described them, caused particular trouble, especially when celebrating a wedding. 'A murder the same night as a marriage was common, and where we lived became a very rough place.'

John Craig loaned Maggie and James enough money to build their own house on the corner of Front and York Street, directly across from the shipyard. To repay this debt and to 'get on in life' James worked all the hours he could, while Maggie found employment both as a domestic, in the palatial city-centre home of John and Annie Craig at 2105 Madison Avenue, and as a cleaner at the offices of the Iron Works which was next door to the shipyard.

James had always wanted to remain his own master and it is perhaps surprising that he worked for almost four years at the Craig shipyard before trying to get a place on one of the trading ships that meander across the Great Lakes. By ill fortune he missed the boat that was supposed to take him to Duluth and, perhaps too embarrassed to ask for his old job back, he went to work as a labourer in the Malleable Iron Works. This, though, as he admits in his journal, was 'much against my will'.

The Malleable was a major enterprise, then employing more than five hundred men. Yet here again Lough soon proved his worth. Within a short period James was given a foreman's job in charge of all the outside work. While this meant extra money, it also caused obvious rancour with 'Tommy', the man he had replaced and who had been effectively demoted. Tommy tried to get Lough the sack by deliberately mixing various grades of pig iron and then informing the works manager, Mr Helm, that the new foreman had ruined the delivery.

James had expected something like this to happen, so that when Helm shouted and whistled for him to come over, he stood his ground. When the manager eventually came over and asked Lough if he had not heard him calling, James replied thus:

'I did hear you, but I don't answer anyone who calls as you did. That is the way we call on our dogs in Scotland and believe me, Mr Helm, I want you to know that I am not a dog. I am an honest man. The noblest work of God'.

This phrase sums up all that Lough stood for and believed in. He might have been sacked on the spot, yet regardless of what that would have meant to a man who was desperate to improve his lot, he chose to speak out and say what he thought. The supervisor was impressed and listened as Lough explained how the pig iron had probably come to be corrupted. Far from losing his job, James was promoted and that day won the respect and friendship of Mr Helm.

Thereafter he was given plenty of overtime – and was always available for more and happy to take on other work, such as the painting of the works' huge chimney stacks. Along with Maggie's income from cleaning they soon amassed a tidy sum. But the entire amount was almost lost when they lodged it in the safe of the Iron Works on the very night that the Malleable burnt down. After three days of worry, when they were convinced all their savings had gone up in smoke, the twisted metal of the safe was recovered from the shell of the factory. Miraculously its contents, including the Loughs' precious dollars, were all intact. After this James and Maggie took the advice of John Craig and deposited their money in an account at the First National Bank.

In 1893 an economic panic, sparked by the great Pullman Strike, caused widespread unemployment and another run on the banks. Lough was one of only three workers kept on at the Malleable during the stoppage and made more money because of it. He was an obvious target for those who were unemployed and destitute. 'Hundreds of idle, desperate men stood outside the entrance of our works and no man or woman was safe who had five dollars in his possession.' Many houses were broken into and each night James slept with a six-chamber revolver under his pillow and a large pistol and chopping axe at his bedside.

Yet in spite of this Maggie, petrified that the First National Bank would fail, insisted that James withdraw all of their money which they then hid under their kitchen carpet. After a warning from John Craig that wherever they hid the cash, robbers would find it and then kill the both of them, Maggie and James moved the money to the safest place they could think of – in a jar under the chicken run at the back of their property.

Weeks later, when they went to recover the jar they found that the damp earth had all but eaten away every dollar bill. Luckily for James and Maggie their friend and cousin John Craig came to their rescue and as a director of the bank managed to salvage the shreds of bills that had retained their serial numbers. Virtually all of their hard-earned cash was saved.

Five years after arriving in America – and true to the word she gave on the first night she spent in Toledo – Maggie and the children departed for Eyemouth. Where four children had come, five returned, baby Jimmy having been born in Ohio in 1893.

James went to New York and watched as his family sailed away on board the *SS Ethiopia*. He was not convinced that Maggie had done the right thing and had decided to stay in America for a while in case she changed her mind and came back again.

On his way back to Ohio, James Lough fell ill with a fever. He took to his bed and as he lay there he saw the face of his wife and felt the warmth of her breath on his hand. James checked the time on his bedside clock and later found it to have been the exact moment when the *SS Ethiopia* had struck an iceberg in the North Atlantic. 'It was then my wife said to our children "What will your father think when he hears the news that we are all at the bottom of the sea?" So Spirit acts on Spirit. It was at that moment that Maggie – my dear wife – came so near to me on that Sunday afternoon.'

By rights, James should have been made a childless widower that day. The *Ethiopia* was stuck in mid-Atlantic, listing heavily and taking in water from a huge gash in the prow. Maggie Purves refused to take to the lifeboats with the other women and children. The eldest boy Robert, at fifteen years of age, was classed as a 'man' and she would have had to leave him behind.

Somehow the ship stayed afloat, and after plugging the hole with bags of flour from the hold, the captain managed to navigate a slow passage across the ocean to Glasgow.

If Maggie had previously harboured any doubts about staying in Scotland for good, her mind was now wholly made up. James, on learning what had befallen his family, likewise decided that fate was calling him back to Eyemouth.

James said his goodbyes to John Craig, Annie Losee and their children George, John Franklyn, Kate and Mary and also to his own brother-in-law Willie Purves, who alone of the original trio would put roots down in America, and then made his way to New York and home. Again, as with their arrival in Toledo and John Purves' hasty departure for Berwickshire, James did not tell anyone in Eyemouth of his intentions, and arrived back on November 22nd 1895.

The only person in their house was John Craig's aunt Sarah Craig-Robertson, then a very old woman of almost ninety. It was washing day and Maggie was away with a big load to the bleaching green at the far end of the town. Maybe the shock of seeing her husband when she made her way back with her basket pushed Maggie into labour because, as James relates, 'Doctor Forsyth paid a visit to that famous place Tam Stone where all the bairns in Eyemouth come from, and that night our third boy, George, was born'. Tam Stone – or 'Stane' – is the name of a rocky outcrop in Eyemouth Bay and, in a local corruption of the story of the Stork, he is said to bring children with him any time he visits a house. It was a perfect homecoming present for James – and, incidentally, quite a commentary on the times that Maggie, so heavily pregnant, thought nothing of taking a large load of heavy laundry to and from the distant washing ground.

There is no doubt that James Lough would have preferred to stay in Ohio. But his heart always belonged to Maggie and a large part of hers was wedded to Eyemouth. America, though, had been good to them, and they now had enough to pay off all of the bills which they had left outstanding.

The couple had long fancied a house on George Street and bought number seventeen with £250 ready money. It would be the home of the Loughs and their offspring until the dying years of the twentieth century. By a quirk of coincidence, one of so many in this story, it was the next house along from St Ella's Wynd, home to George Craig and his family. James thought much of his neighbours. They too were direct descendants of the Coldingham weaving family. 'They are amongst the foremost fishermen,' Lough would write, 'not only in our town but in our county.' Many years later, in 1959, George Craig's grandson George Craig Aitchison married James Lough's great-granddaughter Jasmin Lough Dale Waddell. Of their four children, I was the third born.

Even after buying seventeen George Street, which he would expand by adding a third-floor tier to accommodate a very large, extended family,

James still had plenty of money left over. Eyemouth was as poor on his return as it had been when he left and Lough was now considered to be a man of great wealth. He didn't much fancy going back to the sea as a fisherman, but he did buy a fishing boat which he managed and sometimes sailed in. Lough's main aim, though, was to set himself up as a coastal trader. Perhaps recalling how close he had come to entering the merchant marine on the Great Lakes, James searched for a small ship to give him a start in business and eventually bought a sailing vessel called *Achilles*.

He hawked himself around and won contracts running coal and timber from northern England to Scotland. It was the start of an enterprise that would provide employment and a decent living not just for Lough but for three of his four sons. His eldest boy Robert, known to all as 'the engineer', was a self-taught mechanic with no equal around the coast. Jimmy and John became adept and experienced seamen, able to navigate and handle the boat in all weathers. George, who suffered ill health and was not suited to a life at sea, stayed on shore.

The boys were still in short trousers when Lough acquired the *Achilles*. Only Robert was old enough to join the crew, which was otherwise made up of James's own elderly father Robert, Jim Windram who had married James's eldest daughter Agnes and two other Eyemouth men. Lough is curiously quiet about the fate of that boat, only mentioning that after two years they 'lost my old sailing ship *Achilles* at Newbiggin on the Northumberland coast'. The family history adds a little bit more detail in the form of a rhyme that was much laughed about in the aftermath of the sinking and which uses the nicknames, or tee-names, of the individuals involved. Few Eyemouth men were called by the name recorded on their birth certificate. James Lough was 'Young Seabreeze'. His father Robert was, of course, 'Old Seabreeze', while Jim Windram, for reasons unknown, was referred to as 'Fairy'.

> *It was the Old Achilles*
> *That sailed the wintry sea*
> *She came ashore at Newbiggin*
> *Newbiggin-by-the-sea*
> *Old Seabreeze was the skipper*
> *Young Seabreeze ran it ashore*
> *And Fairy he lay down below*
> *Snoring like a bore*

Lough, an accomplished skipper, misjudged the channel and rammed his vessel on to the rocks. Luckily for James he had managed to save two hundred pounds from the coal trade, and after selling his fishing boat and all its gear he managed to finance the building of one of the new class of steam drifters. To the great delight of his wife, the vessel was named the *SS Maggie Purves*. Two prosperous years later James added another, much bigger boat. Its name could have been predicted by any who knew the family. It was called the *SS Maggie Lough*.

Business went well. By 1912 both puffers were clear of debt, and James Lough's interests steamed ahead. His sons were growing up strong, fit, able and attractive. And his daughters – Agnes, Jean and Jamesena – were all married off. The family were staunch Methodists and every Sunday they marched through Eyemouth from 17 George Street up along Church Street to the Smiddy Brae and then on to the little chapel in Albert Road. The girls were members of the choir which welcomed a new minister, the Rev Tom Dale from Yorkshire, to the town in 1907. Soon afterwards Mr Dale's brother Jack came to Eyemouth for a visit. Jamesena Lough was immediately smitten. Jack Dale was equally infatuated, and after a period of suitable courtship the pair were married in a 'big wedding' in the town. The officiating minister was, naturally, the Reverend Tom Dale.

Jack Dale, a lecturer in mechanical engineering, took his new bride away to England, but returned in the late 1920s after falling ill with tuberculosis. He would live out his days in air that was healthier than the industrial grime of northern England. Jack and Jamesena had only one child – a girl, Margaret Purves Lough Dale - who had been born in Darlington in 1913. Born, in yet another ironic twist, in the town's Craig Street. Young Peggy lapped up the stories that were told around the hearth by the old worthies – and she was a favourite of James Lough who delighted in telling her of his time in America and of all that had befallen the family, both before and since.

Peggy helped her ailing father in a photography business which he set up in the town and amassed a huge collection of images of 'Auld-Haimoothe'. She also inherited a family heirloom in the shape of a bale of linen. Handed on by her aunt Agnes who, in turn, was given it by Sarah Craig-Robertson, the linen had been woven in the eighteenth century by their Craig forebears, then of Coldingham.

Had it not been for the assassin's bullet that started the War to

End All Wars in a backstreet in Sarajevo, perhaps the Lough empire might have grown to rival that of John Craig: one building great ships, the other trading in them. But the coming of conflict put an end to the coastal trade, and the Admiralty commandeered the *Maggie Lough* to work as a supply vessel for the Grand Fleet. James Lough and his sons, Robert, James – and later John – went as part of the package.

A few months before they were ordered to Scapa Flow, and just days after the outbreak of hostilities, Lough claims that the *Maggie Lough* was boarded by German sailors. James himself was in Eyemouth at the time with his other vessel, leaving the *Maggie Lough* under the command of his son Robert, 'the engineer'. They were running a cargo of coal from Grangemouth to Stonehaven but were obliged to anchor in Largo Bay off the Firth of Forth because of a night-time black-out when, according to Robert, two German submariners came on board and, after first appearing to be British officers, drew revolvers and demanded to be shown where Leven was on the Fife coast. The men left without firing a shot, and after the Loughs reported the incident to the authorities, the Firth of Forth was closed for two days.

There is no firm historical evidence to substantiate Robert Lough's claim that his little ship was boarded by Germans, but a U-boat, U-21, was operating in North Sea waters and along the Forth at this time.

Two weeks after the incident with the submarine, whilst running along the Berwickshire coast with a cargo of slabs en route to Methil, one of James Lough's crew sighted a periscope. Though they didn't know it, this was the U-21. James immediately reported what they had witnessed to the coastguard at Eyemouth but this time their story was not believed. On the very next day, September 5th 1914, the first British ship to be sunk by a torpedo was attacked by the U-21 and sunk off St Abbs Head. *HMS Pathfinder* went down with the loss of 259 lives. Only eleven survivors were picked up.

James Lough and his sons didn't have an easy time of it during the Great War. As non-combatants they were often badly treated by the naval authorities, and were asked time and again to venture out for no good reason in conditions that should have kept them in port. They did their duty, even to the extent of sailing through a minefield in Scapa Flow because, like the Charge of the Light Brigade during the Crimean

War, they had been given the wrong orders but were instructed none-theless to do as they were bid.

The work, the weather, the poor rations and the stress all took their toll. But while James and the three boys battled on, Maggie Purves began to fail. In May 1918 three telegrams arrived in quick succession in Orkney:

'Mother very sick. Will wire you later.'

'Mother serious, you better come home.'

'Come home at once, mother much worse.'

Maggie Purves died at the age of sixty-two on May 22nd 1918. Though James lived a further twenty-two years, it was the beginning of the end for him as well. 'It has been made very plain to me that when Mother passed away our defence was broken and ill or ills have befallen our home ever since. We have been unable to ward them off.'

Very soon after the death of Maggie, James's eldest son, Robert, fell seriously ill and was sent home from Fair Isle. Delirious with fever, the engineer went missing and his father spent almost a week scouring the country before locating his son in a Perth hospital. The eldest of the Lough boys never fully recovered and died at the age of forty-four in 1924. The same fate had already befallen his youngest brother John, who came down with a similar mystery illness that likewise caused him to waste away. John died in 1923, aged just twenty-three. And the only American-born member of the family was also afflicted by a torpor which scythed through him. Jimmy Lough died in 1929 at the age of thirty-six.

As their niece, my grandmother, Peggy Purves Lough Dale Waddell, has said, 'All three of the boys were big strong men, but they all died as though infected with TB or something worse, much worse. It was said in the family that it must have been a German poison or gas or some such that caused them all to die'.

Only George, who did not go to sea, was left of Lough's four sons. Lacking the will to carry on alone, James sold off the *Maggie Lough*. In any case he had made his money and his mark on the world. All the years of thrift, of sacrifice and of making-do-and-mend now yielded enough for a comfortable retirement. His proud boat, though, did not end its days as a pensioned-off puffer. The *SS Maggie Lough* is alleged to have been spotted by a film producer and made it into the movies as the 'star' of the 1950s Ealing Comedy *The Maggie*.

James Lough often idled away his afternoons at the head of the pier in Eyemouth, watching the fishing fleet come in or go out, admiring the view, perhaps gossiping with other old worthies, including his brother-in-law John Purves – the man who had been an émigré for just three months. On one such occasion the Free Kirk minister in the town, Rev John Millar, parked himself at James's side. They spoke at length of Lough's life of adventure, his achievements and the desperate sadness of the loss of three of his boys and especially of his beloved wife Maggie Purves. As he got up to leave Mr Millar turned round and said, 'Man cannae fathom God'. To a quizzical look he carried on, 'Do you think, Jim, that Maggie could have stood seeing her boys die like that? She would have broken her heart. It is a blessing, a true blessing that she was called by God first'.

James's love for Maggie had been all-consuming. It eclipsed all other things. He would gladly have stayed in the United States if she had allowed it, yet gave up his obvious liking for the life he had carved out in Ohio for the wife who yearned for home.

There is much in the writing of James Lough that reflects and complements the thoughts of John Craig. Both were American in outlook even though only one was American by birth. Both were Scottish in grit and honesty, even though only one was Scottish by birth.

James Lough longed to return to his old home in Toledo, and with enough money in his pocket he did so in 1922 - and then again in 1928 when at the age of seventy-one he bought a railroad ticket that took him from New York right across to the west coast via Canada. He made many stops to visit those of the Berwickshire diaspora, usually arriving unannounced, to be greeted with little surprise by people he might not have seen for thirty years or more – 'Oh it's yourself Jimmie, would you not come in?'

James ended up in California where he renewed his acquaintance with John Craig's two sons, John Franklyn and George. John Franklyn had started work in the Toledo yard just after James Lough arrived in America and their relationship was strong and friendly. John Franklyn, though he had his father's business acumen, suffered ill health and he was warned by his doctor that he risked death if he continued to live in the harsh Ohio climate. The medic suggested a move to Arizona which prompted the reply, 'I doubt if I will build many ships in the desert!' Instead John Franklyn looked to the western seaboard and in 1907 the family sold the Toledo yard for $550,000 and secured a new base at Long Beach, California. They were enticed to do so by the local populace who wanted the industry and energy of the Craig family. Indeed a subscription was raised to purchase the land on which the new shipyard was built. Thousands would eventually find work there on what was the first major industrial enterprise in Long Beach. Many of these employees followed the Craigs from Ohio in a specially chartered train which brought the workers and their families out west.

The Long Beach yard, which runs along from the famous Pacific sands which give the city its name, mushroomed and expanded as the years rolled on. Yachts and yawls and pleasure craft of all shapes and sizes were built along with commercial ships, naval vessels and submarines which saw service in both world wars.

In 1926 John Franklyn Craig, by then a successful and wealthy businessman in his own right, journeyed to Europe where he visited James Lough and his family in Eyemouth and took photographs of the original Craig home in Coldingham. It was during this visit that the possibility of Lough's son Jamie, who had been born in Toledo in 1893, emigrating to work with his American cousins in California was enthusiastically mooted. Two years later James Lough returned to Ohio to obtain the necessary citizenship papers for Jamie and then trekked across the continent to spend several weeks with the Craigs in Long Beach. James was a talented lay preacher and he clearly impressed the local Methodist congregation which delegated him to represent them at a world Sunday school forum in Los Angeles.

Lough returned to Scotland brimful of stories. He also carried with him the citizenship papers which would allow his son to move to Long Beach to work with his Craig cousins. Tragically young Jamie who, along with his two brothers Robert and John, had suffered ill health since their service in the merchant fleet during the Great War, died within months of his father's return home. No further visits were made by the offspring of James Lough to the descendants of John Craig until I arrived in California in the spring of 2004. James Gourlay Craig junior, the great-grandson of John Craig, gave me, the great-great grandson of James Lough, the type of welcome and showed the generosity that our forefathers would have heartily approved of.

John Craig and Annie Losee had remained in Toledo when their two sons made the move west. Of their two daughters, Kate had married

Don Douglas (founder of the aircraft company which later became McDonnel Douglas) while Mary married a Michigan businessman called Alfred Merrell. It was their daughter Ruth Craig Merrell who would write Captain Craig's biography, *Episodes of My Life*, in 1928.

Retirement in Toledo brought little rest for John Craig. The man who had overseen the construction of 107 vessels on the Great Lakes now took an interest in a huge number of organisations. He was President of the Toledo Steamship Company, the Adams Transportation Company and the Monroe Transportation Company. He continued as director of the First National Bank and was Vice-President of the Toledo Metal Wheel Company, a trustee of the Flower Hospital and was a member of the Toledo Yacht Club and the Society of Naval Architects and Engineers of New York. Like James Lough he was an avowed teetotaller and became President of the United Dry Campaign of Lucas County.

But the biggest presidential office of all nearly came John Craig's way when he agreed to let his name go forward for nomination on the Republican ticket for President of the United States of America. It would have marked the apogee of the American dream for a remarkable son of Scotland. Eventually Craig stood aside to support the candidacy of fellow-Ohioan William Taft who was elected as the twenty-seventh President in November 1908.

Like James Lough, John Craig protected his pennies, but also allowed himself extravagances - like the great trip to Europe and the Holy Land which he took with his wife in 1904. The letters Craig sent back, and which are included here, are an early if completely politically-incorrect travelogue. They also provide some perceptive analysis of the power of religious fanaticism, and the possibility of the rise of Islamic fundamentalism.

John Craig was honoured by his family on the occasion of his sixty-seventh wedding anniversary. The centrepiece of the party was the presentation by his granddaughter Ruth Craig Merrell of *Episodes of My Life*, a biography which she had worked on with Craig and with his family and friends for many months. Part of the information had come from James Lough, who was delighted to help when he met Ruth during his visit to America in 1928.

Indeed the project sparked the thought in James Lough's mind that he should perhaps do something similar. It is totally in keeping with his character that he didn't tell anyone in the family what he was doing, even when the tightly scrawled 113-page manuscript was finished. Instead he sealed it up and secretly sent it overseas to Ruth Craig Merrell.

The lives of John Craig and James Lough are intertwined in many ways. They were both principled and both had loving and strong partners. They both believed in their own purpose and in the power of God. They both had a tremendous desire to better themselves and provide for their families. And they both lived very long and eventful lives. John Craig died peacefully in Toledo on 14th January 1934 at the age of ninety-five. James Lough slipped away after illness had struck him down at the age of eighty-three, six years later on October 14th 1940 – coincidentally on the anniversary of Black Friday.

The links between Lough and Craig would never have come to light had it not been for the sharp interest of their descendants. Patricia Smethurst, the great-great-granddaughter of Peter Craig – who had made it rich in the Californian Gold Rush – was the first to establish that both men had left written biographies. She also pieced together the tortuous family trees which allowed us to link up with John Craig's great-grandson Jim, who lives in fine style in Long Beach, California. His fourth cousins include both Patricia Smethurst of Maine and Peggy Purves Lough Dale Waddell of Eyemouth. At the time of writing that grand old lady has just celebrated her ninety-first birthday. As a child she had sat spellbound listening to stories from her 'Goff' James Lough of his time in Toledo, of their American relatives, of the happy times and the sad times, of his wife and of his children. Peggy never wrote these stories down, and nor did she know that her beloved grandfather, a man lacking in any formal education whatsoever, had committed his own life story to paper in 1929.

When the memoirs eventually surfaced, after seventy-five years, so many of the incidents James related were familiar to the family. They had been told and retold in a rich oral tapestry woven from the remarkable memory of Peggy Dale. Time and again she would fill in the ending of a story from Lough's manuscript before I had had a chance to finish reading it. One incident was particularly poignant. Towards the end of his memoirs James Lough relates how, in the summer of 1928, he had been wandering along the harbour when a young boy slipped and fell from the quayside. With no other volunteer willing to dive in, James, at the age of seventy-one, plunged in and rescued the boy. When I read the story out my grandmother sat bolt upright and seized my arm. 'I was there. I was walking with Goff. He handed his jacket to me when he dived in.'

Peter Aitchison
Eyemouth, May 2004

EPISODES
OF MY
LIFE

JOHN CRAIG

*As Told in my Ninetieth Year
to my Granddaughter
Ruth Craig Merrell
and Compiled by her*

*This book is compiled and lovingly dedicated
to my Grandfather and Grandmother in honour
of their sixty-seventh wedding anniversary.*

R.C.M.

One hundred copies printed for private distribution only.
November 4, 1928

Foreword

In a recent visit to the home of my grandfather, now fore score years and ten, I felt anew the power of his personality and found him as in the days of my youth a most fascinating story teller. For many, many years in whatever group, large or small, of strangers or friends that he has been placed he has soon been marked for his geniality and his entertaining stories told in his inimitable manner. That his descendants and friends may have in some tangible form the tales they have so often heard and enjoyed I have compiled these stories as he told them to me in the spring of his ninetieth year.

He is today as keen and alert and as interested in people and the affairs of the world as he was when he cast his first ballot for Lincoln. There is a spring to his step and a twinkle in his eye, and a spirit of loving kindness and understanding emanates from his smile that is joyous to behold. To prove to him that others than those of us bound to him 'by ties of sanguininity' (as he would say), see, feel, and appreciate his remarkable virility of mind, body, and spirit I here print the letter for one who has for years come in contact with the best our country had to offer in brains and brawn. Being a medical man he knows the physical side of the average American who has passed the four score mark and being a statesman he has seen the minds of big men at work. His contacts have been so numerous and varied that these words should convey to my Grandsire the realisation of the fact that it is for due and just reason that we, his kith and kin, are so proud of him.

Truly the life of John Craig is an inspiration as is that of his ever-present helpmate, my Grandmother. They have made so much out of their time on this old world! They have faced life so squarely. They have made the utmost out of each new situation. They have grown along together in patience, tolerance, and loving kindness, glorying in the good to be found in this world and ever striving to make it a better place for man-kind to live in. It is a happy business, me thinks, to ponder on lives like these.

RUTH CRAIG MERRELL
Long Beach, California, September, 1928

Royal S. Copeland, New York
C.W. JURNEY, SECRETARY

United States Senate
WASHINGTON, D.C.

250 West 57th Street
New York

July 9, 1928

My dear Mrs. Merrell:

We were very sorry to miss seeing you in Toledo. But really we had a very wonderful time there. I am always glad to see your father, as you know, but to meet your Grandfather was an added privilege.

I consider Mr. Craig the most remarkable man of his age I have ever had the privilege of knowing. For years I have preached the doctrine – "Live to be a hundred". I have always added, however, that it isn't worth while to live a hundred years unless you are effective and useful at that age.

Here is a man, 90 years of age, with all of his faculties and possessed of as keen a mind as I have ever met. I said to him that I hope he will permit me to come sometime just to talk with him all day. I meant every word of what I said.

There are few men now living who were mature adults at the time of Lincoln, Everett, Horace Greely, Tweed, and other men of that period: some good – some bad. Your Grandfather knew them all and has such a vivid recollection of them and tells his story in such an interesting way that he is irresistible.

I was not talking for the press, as you humorously suggested, but telling the truth when I said that I thought Mr Craig is the most remarkable man of his years I have ever met. If I can add to this in any way, please commend me.

I am sorry we did not see you the other day, but hope to have the pleasure before long.

With kindest regards to you and yours,

Cordially,

Mrs Thos. R. Merell
1242 Cedar Avenue,
Long Beach, California

Royal S. Copeland

Scotch Ancestry

Coldingham, Berwickshire, Scotland, was the birth place of my ancestors – my father and grandfather, both carrying the name George Craig. You see it is an old Scotch custom that the first son in a family should be named after the paternal grandfather and as every oldest son of our family until I came along was born in the same stone house in Coldingham for two hundred years back, you will find many Georges, Johns and Peters on our family tree.

When father (George Craig) was about eighteen years of age in 1827 he sailed for Quebec on a ship of three hundred tons with about three hundred passengers and was three months in making the voyage – got a job at once and in a short time earned enough money to send for his brother Peter. They sent for John and later sent for the whole family. All soon moved from Quebec to New York City where my grandfather and grandmother died of cholera in 1834 and were buried in New York beside their babe. This left Peter and George, (my father) and John (a very young lad) and Sophie (who afterwards married a Mr. Porter) and Jeannette (who married Dr. Graten and lived in Stockton, California) and Christiana (who married Mr. Trumpore), to shift for themselves.

The family held together till in '49 when the boys got the fever to go to California in the 'gold rush'. The two eldest cast lots to see who would go West. Peter won the die so my father stayed to take care of his brothers and sisters. When casting lots the brothers made a bargain to stand for three years that one-half of whatever was made by the lucky one would belong to the stay-at-home brother and his family.

Peter went to California and became immensely rich, while father worked as a ship sawyer and at jobs in the coal yards, to support the families. About three years later Peter returned to New York to see his brothers and sisters and offered my father a small amount of cash for the family's use. Father refused the gift, recalling the bargain made that night a few years before, but Peter denied the existence of any such arrangement and the brothers parted their ways – Peter going on to the old country to spend his money and visit his married sister.

James Lough has told you the story of Peter meeting his sister Sarah, whom he had not seen for nearly forty years. He was 'speaking to Maggie' (his wife), as he calls it, about that time. Maggie was at her aunt's (and my aunt's) house the night Peter appeared. Father was very prominent in the Caledonian Society in those days and befriended many a Scotch seaman while his ship was getting underway so he wouldn't have to go back to the old country.

My mother's maiden name was Catherine Campbell. She was born in Grampian Hills, Scotland. She and father were married in New York City and I was one of a family of four; Catherine, Jeannette and Jean being my sisters. Catherine died in childhood. Jeanette married Alex R Linn of Detroit. Jean married James Gourlay and both have gone to their long resting place. I have often heard my father say 'Twas a bitter stormy night, the night that lad was born'. He was referring to my advent for I was born between the twenty-fourth and twenty-fifth of December, 1838 – and still am permitted to enjoy this wondrous sphere.

There are living today four generations of John Craigs, all American born, their birth states stretching across this great country of ours, as I was born in New York, my son in Michigan, my grandson in Ohio and my great-grandson in California.

Early Influences

Now we were talking about bringing up children, and a great deal of my success is due to the early training my mother gave me. She was very conscientious about training me to a system. Every day when I came home from school I had to learn my lessons first, and then recite them to my mother until I had them perfect. After I had read them over once or twice I usually knew them so it was not a long task, and then I had to bring up wood, no coal for us in those days, and do the errands, buy needs or anything under my mother's instructions. Then I had to learn 1 to 5 verses of the Bible every day. If there was any time left I could play. Just as regular as day came I went through this schedule till she died. System! Now I wouldn't last a week without a system. I get up at five, take one half hour gymnastics, go to bathroom and take one-half teaspoonful sal-soda, clean my teeth – they are all my own you know, not a pair of these fancy removable ones that an old fellow my age usually is wearing. Yes, my teeth have stood by me all these years and seen hard service too. Then I wash and go down stairs. Read the paper and eat at 7:00 o'clock and sit in the front parlour window with your grandmother and just sort of meditate there a few minutes till Cliff (Whitmore) comes along. He and I have walked down town together every morning for nineteen years if the weather is nice. We used to walk home at 4:30 but now he has to wait for daily balance at the bank till 5:00 or after. So we quit and I come alone. Cliff says I'm more like a father to him than any man on the face of the earth. I've always liked him for he always has been economical, go beyond that and call it stingy, till now he's liberal but he's got it to spend. I've lent him up to $20,000 that's why I'm like a father I suppose.

But I must get back to my text. It's early training that counts – my mother was always regular with me as long as she lived – she died when I was thirteen – yes, father married again but not for a long time after she died. After she died we boarded with a family named Mellis for two years and then my sister Jean begged father to let her go to housekeeping. We had an aunt in a thread and needle store and she was successful so she took in Jeanette, and Jean and I and father lived together. Then Jean was married (to James Gourlay) and soon I was married and Dad came to me one day and said, 'John, *I'm* going to get married,' and I said 'Father what in the world are you thinking of? You have three homes and welcome in all of them'. He said, 'That is just it! I want a home of my *own*. Now I'm not going to be a fool and marry some little girl and bring children into the world and make hell for you and all of the rest of yours. And if your mother is looking over the battlement of heaven she'd say tonight, 'George marry Mary, for she has dandled you in her arms many times.' So that took the wind out of me, and I said, 'Do you remember what you said to me when I got married? "You've made your bed now you'll have to lie in it." '

She was a Welsh woman about father's age. When I was a baby she had rented one floor and we another in the same house. Nobody lived in houses by themselves those days, two to five family dwellings. So our families had been acquainted more or less for many, many years. She had about enough property to be independent and father had about enough to make him independent. They came West, went to Maine, to Scotland, to Wales, travelling and were like two peas in a pod. She died suddenly in two days and he mourned faithfully for her but in a different manner than for our mother. His grandchildren were a thorn in her flesh, and she felt, took away his affection: they lived together thirty years, and each would do what they were minded to. Oh, he lived five or ten years after she died and he made his home with Aunt Jeannie and divided his time up with all of us.

When a boy, we lived in the section of New York City called the Dry Dock. The city was divided up into settlements; here would be a Scotch colony, there an Irish colony and over yonder the Jews. Each settlement had a colloquial name.

Father worked in the ship yards, then a coal yard and then was a seller of lumber for a New York firm. He earned about $2.00 a day and we never stood in a soup line either, though many a $5.00 foreman did. He quit business when at the age of fifty-six and was a gentleman of leisure and travel. I have always had great respect for my father and his ability. He would have made a big mark in the world I feel sure had he dared to accept the opportunities offered him. But on account of the responsibilities devolving on him being the oldest of the family and the care of his sick parents and all his young brothers and sisters, he could never take the chances that would have led him to bigger fields. He always said he was great by association as most all the great men of his century were born in 1809 – Lincoln, Gladstone, and Webster and many others. He had a string of some twenty or more he could name.

My father was brought up a Presbyterian and after he got married he got it into his head that the Baptists were nearer Christians, then he got it into his head that Disciples were nearer Christians according to the gospels.

So father was not anything, in fact was about half a Spiritualist. He would go to meetings and see things he believed couldn't be known to anybody but himself, and he would believe in the spirits. He and I had an experience with the Fox girls of Rochester. We lived in Green Point and a friend of ours, the superintendent of Safe Company heard that the Fox girls were great. So father and I went up there to hear the rappings. I was fifteen, just old enough to reason on subjects I wasn't taught right. Father was holding the door and knocks would come on it and he'd open the door and nobody would be there, and he couldn't understand.

'Say John,' he says, 'Let's you and I try it at the table'. We went to the little table in the kitchen and he began to say, 'If any spirits are present, please manifest by moving to me.' They put plates under the legs of the table and when the table moved toward him he says to me, 'What are you moving the table for, John?' I says, 'I ain't, father.'

Apparently we had a communication from my mother. My sisters had gone to Detroit to visit our Aunt Wilkie and we had no letter for three or four weeks and we were worried about them. The rapping told us the cholera was bad. Sisters comparatively worn out from helping with the dying. In a week when a letter came it was a facsimile of the information we had gathered that night. Another time he had gone to a meeting in New York and the medium had a message for father though he didn't know anyone in the meeting. The message was from one, James Doe, a baker from Eyemouth, Scotland, a respectable young man that everybody had admired. There was a Miss Allen that had three brothers, wood merchants of considerable means, that lived near the bake shop and unknown to the brothers, Miss Allen and James Doe were keeping company. They threatened to disown her unless she gave this man up, and he disappeared out of Eyemouth the next few days and nobody know where he had gone. It was revealed to him then what had become of James Doe. He was buried in a silver mine in California. The medium also revealed how two old sailors from Eyemouth were lost and he heard from them the same night. These were all Scotch names that the New York medium couldn't have manufactured and my father certainly was not thinking of them as they had not entered his head for years. All this tended to make father pretty much of a spiritualist. More or less he'd go to all such meetings till he died. He agreed with me if possible he'd come back tho he never has in all the years I've been living. There's some power we can't understand, but even the spiritualists haven't found the key.

Years later a girl from Georgia was a famous medium, so father, my son Georgie, a Dr. Corville and I went down to see that girl and a piano would follow her around the room. Then the doctor's nephew, a 250 pounder, Bob Herring by name, said he'd sit on the piano. He did and it would follow her with the extra weight! And I said, 'Give me that power. I'm a shipbuilder and I'd like to have that power to pull loads of timber around.' And she said, 'Oh no I can't ever do that; when I apply it to jobs of that sort my power leaves me.'

This altered father's whole life. He couldn't feel sure what it was all about. Some little thing would kick over the possibility of belief and that left him a 'doubting Thomas' and affected his whole life. There is a power I feel sure that we'll learn to find and will put it to good use to help man. There's a connection from mind to mind that we haven't discovered. The only satisfaction I find is in faith. There is a God that leads and guides this world by means we do not know but certain things are accomplished through it. Now, take our Civil War. Slavery got obnoxious to half of the country. We wanted the question settled for all times as it was against all humanity. But for a while we were whipped and continued to get whipped until the emancipation proclamation. After that *open expression of our faith* in our cause we were successful. It looks as though God works in mysterious way his wonders to perform. We had and have freedom of slaves for the world by a man voicing his belief.

My Apprenticeship

You asked me how I happened to get interested in ships. Well, I was one of the youngest students ever admitted to New York Free Academy and my school chum's father was Captain of a schooner which sailed from New York to Apalachicola, a prominent town in Florida, his trip occupying about six weeks. His father's thoughts were that the sea was the place for a young man that had any 'get-up-and-get-into-him,' or hopes to advance in the battle of life. Everytime the boat came to New York this chum and I were on her every spare moment, from the time she docked till she sailed and his father was ever preaching to us the benefit of sea-going life. The owners of his boat were building a boat to make a captain of his first mate who was only 24 years old, and the second mate was going to be first mate and he was only 20 years old. Well, that got the idea of following the mast in my head so strongly that I continually harped upon it at home till father had to take cognizance of it and said, 'Young man, I don't want you to keep harping of sea-going life here, and make us unhappy combating your notions. But if you are determined upon a sea-going life you had better become a ship carpenter and then you can go to sea as an officer and get rid of the drudgery you would have as an apprentice before the mast.' I fell for the idea and he got me a job as apprentice to learn to be a ship carpenter.

I don't think I had been an apprentice more than two or three months when I would have given all my old boots and shoes and thrown in my stockings to be back as a student in the New York Free Academy! But having made my bed I was determined to lie in it, and started to become a perfect ship carpenter and I so excelled because of my education that I was offered a number of positions as carpenter for some East Indies ships. But after I saw the way the sailors lived, and the positions they occupied about the ship it looked no better than slavery, and I didn't want to become a ships carpenter. However, I was almost persuaded to sail on one of the biggest ships clearing New York as I was a pet of a certain captain. But one day I saw him, my hero, drunk and abusing his men with no recourse on their part. I said, 'Salt water shall never wash over me as a slave'. And I determined to get as far as I could in my job but to stay *on shore* with my labors. Had I gone to sea I might have been as successful in anything else, for it was really to a great extent luck that I got in with Mr. Simonson, for he was getting old and I was there to fill the breach. He was a Methodist and my father while not a Methodist just then had been through all those wrinkles and was in with him so he sent me around for the job that rainy day.

I had been with C. and R. Pollion and a great many times when they went to make an estimate they would take me with them and we'd measure what stuff was necessary. My education made me handy on these jobs, so when they got a boat to build they sent me to the loft to help lay her down and the superintendent sneeringly said a 50c man would do as well! That made me mad, so that night I took all the drawings home and made outlines of all the marks, went and got myself a set of mechanical instruments from a second hand store (your father has them now) and got some paper and started to make the drawings. I got started alright but soon couldn't understand any farther what it was all about, so hunted up a draftsman, Bob Stuler from Webb's Shipyard. (By the way, he afterwards became Chief Naval Architect of United States Navy.) I had him give me lessons Tuesday and Friday nights. He charged 75c an hour, that was what he was getting.

So then we started to build on paper. He said, 'Let us commence at the commencement. Here's a man comes to me and wants us to build a boat to carry 1,000 tons, 12 foot water, and she must never draw more than 12 feet and must go 10 miles an hour, so that between the ports we want her to run she can make each leg of the trip in a week. Must do it regularly as I will advertise, and she must keep to schedule. 12 feet draft is a maximum and she must carry 1,000 tons or expenses would eat us up.'

Our first night was a guess. We guessed a boat so long, so wide, and so deep, a certain percent of an imaginary box would accomplish that purpose. Then we went to work to prove what could be accomplished by the dimensions we had concocted, and then we would increase or decrease dimensions till we came to outlines of the boat we believed would do. We then made a drawing necessary for us to lay a boat down in the mold loft, and by the following spring I made up my mind I knew how to do it, and did it when opportunity came along. It was then I built the schooner *Amelia G. Ireland.* That I'll tell you about a little later.

I told the boss I'd rather be outside than in the loft and he said, 'I've a mind to give you a licking. If I had had that chance when a boy I'd have given my toe nails.' There is another episode in connection with that job too. After our boss had contracted for a boat, their first (always had just made repairs up to that time) they called me in the office and said, 'John, we want you to go get a stem for that boat.'

'Where?' says I.

'Anywhere,' says they.

'What shall I pay?' says I.

'Least you have to,' says they.

'I don't know where to go,' groaned I.

'John,' says the boss, 'you know all the timber men around here. Go get it, don't come back till you *do* get it!'

With that I went off and tramped two or three days visiting every timber-getter I'd ever heard of. Then I struck a man under contract with the navy. And I found he had a stem aboard a ship under a lot of timber, but that the timber had to go to the navy, and in order to get that stem out of the navy, I had to get a pass against the Frigate, *North Carolina,* from her commander, as everything in or out was by his orders. First I got an order from the man who owned the stem by giving him what the navy was paying per cubic foot for timber. Then I went and saw the commander at the navy yard and I remember how I argued saucily that the stem never had been ordered by them and therefore did not belong to the navy so that I deserved a permit. But he only laughed at me. I insisted, I followed him like a dog for one-half to three-quarters of an hour, he laughing at me all the while. Finally I said, 'Now commander, we are under contract to build a boat in 63 days and that is the only piece of timber that would fill the bill north of Virginia.'

Then he took hold of one of my ears and said, 'You're a damn persistent little bugger,' and with that called the superintendent, and asked him if they needed that piece. The constructor said they had no use for it and probably never would have as they had two or three pieces laying in the seasoning pond for the navy. Under those conditions he gave me the order. I hurriedly found my man, got aboard the schooner, and signalled my tug. (Before I had called on the commander I had made arrangements for a float-stage with a tug.) I next hied myself to our office and told them of my trouble. They gave me a big vote of thanks, and that little stunt made me of some importance to my employers and gave me a boost in their estimation.

I laugh now for a boy like your brother George, (in his early twenties) tagging around after a man with gold braid all over him and finally teasing the old fellow into giving me what I wanted!

Our Marriage

We got married about that time (Nov.4, 1861) as I had about $600. I had met your grandmother then Annie Eliza Losee, daughter of Peter and Catharine Ann Losee some years before. Along about 1855 we had a great revival of religion and I always was chummy with my college mate Bob Hallock – we went to singing school of Second St. M. E. Church together and he and I became members of Second St. Church at the same time. I was introduced to my wife by Bob's sister at singing school, and from that time she was my girl and I was her fellow. We were both young and she was so young she played with her girlish toys and her mother threatened to show them to me if she did not put them away. Sarah, her eldest sister, had a young lawyer Armour C. Anderson paying attention to her so we made two couples to go to lectures, concerts etc. We often on a Sunday night would leave our own church and go and hear H. W. Beecher, Billy Corbet, Dr. Roach, and any celebrated preacher or Bishop, and by that means heard all the great preachers or lecturers of our time.

I remember the first time I asked her mother to let me take her to the Crystal Palace – we were going alone – and she said, 'John I hardly know about that – you are pretty young to be going out alone. Do you think you are able to bring her back to me all right?' And I promised by all great, good or gracious I would - and then she gave her consent and from that time on I was just like one of her family – and became acquainted with an all her friends and relatives – and it just became an under-standing that when we were old enough we would be married.

We stood up and were witnesses to her sister's wedding – which was about four years before ours – and today she, Sarah Losee Anderson, and her son Peter Anderson who was then a boy two years old are the only living persons who were at our wedding November 4th, 1861 – and today, I don't think either one of us ever regretted that day – and while we have had our differences or ideas and desires yet I do not think either of us ever felt that life apart was ever considered for a moment. We always have respected each other's ideas – but we finally would come to a good understanding and I have no doubt it will continue until we are called from time to eternity.

That was at the beginning of the Civil War and I was placed in the mold loft to lay down the 'Winona,' one of the first of twenty-three gun boats built during the war. I was the pet and sort of private helped of my employers as I have said.

The second year of the war my father was selling lumber for a firm named Decker and Company and he met an old customer named Simonson and father said to him, 'You're pretty old climbing around ships now, why don't you get a young man to help you?' He said he would if he could find an honest one. Then father said, 'I've got a son that would just suit you,' and he said, 'George, send that boy of yours over and let me see him.'

I Start in Business

So the first rainy day I could lay off I went around to see him and he said he was looking for a young fellow that had nerve and ambition and get-up-and-get-to-him. He quizzed me a while and then said, 'My stuff is worth $1200. Give me $600, and we'll be partners'. 'All right,' I said, 'I'm your huckleberry.' I gave him my $600, all I had, and I was in business! In about two years I had $2000 in the bank.

We had a big fire in New York about that time in which about 30 schooners burned. I snooped around and found one that I thought we could rebuild and make money on. So we formed a company and found a captain that wanted a job. The way they sailed boats then differed from now – they all owned in fractions in one-sixteenth to one thirty-second shares, usually by farmers. The captain made the charter and carried the load. First he paid port charges, harbor fees, water, repairs and then divided the remainder in two parts. Captain got the first half and the owners the rest. So we needed a good honest captain or could do nothing with the boat after we conditioned her. When we finished her I owned one-eighth of the ship, and my first dividends came from her. She was a good schooner and there was plenty to do.

Right about that time I got acquainted with the cousin of the Governor of New Jersey, Joel Parker. Every little town in New Jersey had a little ship yard and he came from a place named Barnygat. He had been a contractor in Washington during the war and got it into his head that he was going to fail, so his partner bought him out for $10,000. Bankruptcy law said you had to do that four months ahead of failure, that is they could look back in your book for four months for your reports. He bought 1,000 acres in Maryland, trees, niggers and all, kept the old business going for four months to cover the farm purchase and then failed. I had made an agreement to find an owner for one-half of a boat to be made out of timber on this land. By this time I had been in business two years. I never had created anything by myself and couldn't point to anything and say, 'This is my handiwork.' I decided I knew my business and would build a ship. So I went down there and got the boat, the *Amelia G. Ireland* in frame. We made her in Maryland, on Wycomico Creek. We cut green timber, whip-sawed it on stilts, or bought it from farmers, or paid them to take timber to the saw mill. All the tools we had wouldn't cost $200 then. I took my men with me except the niggers I picked up. No town was there, just a built camp half way between two county seats, Princess Ann and Saukberg, 16 miles apart, and we were eight miles from each. Hearing of the boat, the old partner from Washington came over and tried to demand part owner-ship. Then, you see, I had to stay to protect my friends who taken interest in the boat to help me. I had to fight it through two circuit courts.

Down South

Yes, we got lots of experience down South that year, for we weren't used to their customs and they didn't think much of us Yankees anyhow. I remember that I never felt so insulted in my life as when I was in a man's house down there on a Christmas Day and they had a big bowl of egg-nog on the table. Everyone that came in was offered a glass of Christmas cheer but me. I was just a Northern mud-still, good enough to buy timber from or lend money to. I didn't want it and wouldn't have taken it anyhow, but I didn't like their attitude toward me.

I remember well a couple of big niggers we had down there. They were big fellows, both of them six feet six inches and their names were Rufus Fields and Jim Shields. They came in and wanted a job. 'Where have you been working?' says I. 'Down at Amiseckes.' That was a little town where they had a railroad. 'What wages do you pay?' says they. 'Well, you see that little man over there,' says I, 'he gets $4 and if you do as much as he does you'll get the same pay as he does'.

'How long do you work?' they asked. 'Ten hours,' says I. 'Oh won't that be fun,' says they. 'Why what's the matter?' says I. 'How long have you been used to working over at Amisecke?' 'Fourteen hours,' says they, 'sun up to sun down.' 'Well, I guess you'll get tired enough in 10 hours round here,' I said. 'That's all you need to work.'

I met those fellows in a couple of weeks and asked them how they were getting along. 'Bless you,' they says, 'we do twice as much work here in 10 hours as over there in fourteen!'

One of these fellows was a preacher of the gospel on the side line and one day when I said I was going north next day, he says, 'Mister Craig would you like to do me a favor?' and I said, 'Yes Rufus, if that's possible and within reason.' So he continued, 'When I goes out to preach I sure would like some Congress gaiters.' 'Well,' I says, 'I have about four hours in Philadelphia and I can get you a pair as well as not.' And he says, 'I'll be ever so much obliged.' So I says, 'What size Rufus?' and he replies, 'Large 13 or small 14, Mr Craig.'

Well I went into three or four stores asking for Rufus's gaiters and they thought I was codling them, as they all said 10's were the biggest they'd ever heard of. So poor Rufus had to spread the gospel without the aid of any Congress gaiters.

We had six of the biggest niggers you ever saw down there. We little fellows would put a beam on their shoulders and use them for truck horses. I used to get the New York Times, and I found out they'd do anything I asked to get their hands on that old newspaper. They'd go on a ten-mile errand just to get that paper for pay. When they'd get their hands on one they'd have a party and the one nigger girl that could read would read aloud to the crowd while another girl held the lighter-wood (that is the heart of a pine tree which is almost pure turpentine and burned like a torch.)

I was down there and tied up in that Butler lawsuit I told you about and was going to be down there for at least three months so Grandma came down with your Uncle George, who was three years old. They stayed there till her brother James Losee died in New York and she went home for the funeral. I remember your Grandmother had a great time with George down there although she had a colored boy to take care for him. He was forever climbing around trying to hunt eggs, under the house or any place that he had an idea there was a nest. He just seemed possessed to squeeze the eggs and I remember one time he did it and put his messy hand down on the floor and the print of his little hand dried there and the old lady wouldn't let us clean it up. Then another day Grandma found 'creepers' (she called them) in his head, so she said, 'It must be those niggers!' So Mrs Meyer had them all shaved. You've never seen a funnier, bluer-looking bunch of niggers than they were, with their kinky hair all gone.

Always while we were having dinner old Nehemiah would sit in front of the fire and read the Bible aloud. 'Twas all he could read in the world and I suppose he just knew that by heart. The boys got awful tired of the grub that year: salt pork, fired eggs, oysters, fish, potatoes, chicken and everything you could think of, all on the table at the same time every meal of the day.

One day the boys decided they were going to do something about the food, so as soon as we sat down one said, 'Well, damn it, we haven't any pork tonight.' Another said, 'Well, damn it, we haven't any eggs tonight.' Then another barked, 'Well, damn it, we haven't any chicken tonight.' While the fourth bellowed, 'Well, damn it, we haven't any fish tonight.'

It was a rather embarrassing meal. However, the old fellow said nothing but took the hint and said he'd go out and try and get a mess of squirrels for a change; so one night when they started their song about 'there ain't no pork tonight' in came the cook with a platter full of the long promised fried squirrels. I thought there was a nigger in the woodpile, but ate the food and enjoyed the change but I noticed the old fellow could hardly read the Bible that night. He'd chew and he'd spit and struggle with his words awhile. Then he'd chew and spit some more. This went on till the last fellow was through with his meal when the old man said, 'Well boys, how do you like muskrats?' Oh my! Oh my! They all flew to the door and aroof! Aroof! Up came those rats. I was the only fellow at the table after that on muskrat night. I didn't mind at all and now I'm told they are considered a good food. I see them in Tiedke's market very often.

There was a couple of dogs down there, and it was a pleasure to see the young one try to persuade the lazy old fellow to come and go muskratting. It was too much of an effort for that old fellow, he thought, but the young one would keep on teasing him, 'till finally they'd trot off together. The young dog would stand right at the rat hole and the old one stand off and bark a bit and scare the rats out of the hole. Then the young one could pounce on Mr. Muskrat and enjoy his meal right there.

The old man's niece, Theodosia Disharoon, and her father would walk the five miles from their little place of an evening just to listen to us Yankees talk. Theodosia was the only girl around for miles so the three single men in our crew were always snooking around her; one of my men, Jim Phillip, had had trouble with his wife so he'd sit in a dark corner and mumble to himself all evening, 'I won't do it.' 'You will do it, I'll make you.' 'I'll kill you.' All such oaths came from his corner each evening till he had the boys scared stiff. 'Twas too bad too, for he was a good carpenter and could hue to a line and fit a piece together as nice as you please. They were sitting around talking marriage and the laws and spitting and chewing and smoking one night when it was about dark; suddenly he said, 'I'm tired, guess I'll go to bed.' And with that lifted the wig off his old bald head! In the darkness of the night the little light shining on that bald cranium scared those old Southerners most to death and they scattered to the four winds as fast as they could go. They said afterwards they thought he had killed himself and that if they were found there with him they'd be accused of murder.

Yes, the darky girls were regular cards too. One was always saying, 'Oh Missy Craig, haven't you got some more of that medicine? I've got another of those terrible pains.' Grandma would fix her up some hot drops and she thought 'twas liquor. About twice a week the girl would have some girls down for dinner and right after dinner they'd go out to the quarters and pretty soon you'd hear the greatest lot of giggling and carrying on. Old Nehemiah Allen was determined to find out what caused all this hilarity, so one night he burst in on the girls and there they all sat snuff digging. They had little tin pepper boxes filled with snuff and a little birch stick that they had chewed on till 'twas a little brush. They stirred this little brush in the little tin box and then rubbed it on their gums. I asked them one day what they did it for and they said to preserve their teeth.

I was there from 1864 to Spring of 1866, so that by the time I had completed the ship the war was over and everything was as flat as a pancake – took her to New York – I said, 'Here is you boat,' and they couldn't pay me, but they said, 'Sell it and we'll give you a fat commission.' I couldn't sell it in those times so they passed the hat and I got $250 for my 16 months work.

When I got home Peter was three months old, just big enough to love. Grandpa Losee said that it was *his* child because he cared for my wife while I was gone. Grandma Losee came in one Saturday night soon after I got back and said, 'That child is very sick. John go get a doctor!' I went, of course. Annie hadn't had much experience with babies but the doctor failed to show up that night. Grandpa and Grandma Losee came again on their way to church in the morning. They insisted this time I do go for a doctor and bring him with me. I did and the doctor came and said as soon as he looked at it, 'Baby will die in one and one-half hours,' and he did – cholera infantum. I felt then like going to the dock and jumping in. I had been gone from home all that time, had used up the couple of thousand I had in the bank and now had only $100, a dead baby, and no job or prospects left. But then my wife showed her worth and said, 'John, you must pull yourself together, you need perseverance and pluck.

You're a good mechanic and 'tis true we haven't little Peter but we must get along.' That gave me heart and I resolved to keep going if she could, and luck turned, for when one door closes another one often opens up somehow, and it proved so this time.

Headed West

About this time my sister Jennie's husband, Alex Linn, was down buying tea in New York, and he said, 'I've got an uncle, Robert W. Linn, in Gibraltar, Michigan, that needs you and the work is just what you are looking for.' I wrote to Mr Linn and he wired 'Come on,' so I borrowed a little from Grandpa Losee so I could go to Gibraltar and get the job before somebody else heard of it. I got there and he took me on to finish a schooner, the *Jane Ralston* for him. I lived in his house and he had a store so I got free tobacco and don't suppose I spent a dollar till I left after the boat was launched. He said, 'How much do I owe you?' I said, '$200.' I had been working for him about two months and he said, 'That ain't enough,' and gave me $500. He said, 'Now young man I believe you know how to build boats. With 170 acres of land, my timber, and my influence and your ability and your youth, I think we can get another boat.'

So I went back to New York and packed my family on the train and our household goods on a canal boat within a week and moved to Gibraltar. 'Twas considered way out West in those days. The first boat we built was in 1866. It cost us about $16,000 and our contract called for $20,000 so my share was $2,000 and once more I was up in the world again.

My wife certainly paid dear for that $2,000, for she stuck by me through thick and thin. She made a wonderful sacrifice when she followed me to Gibraltar – leaving New York where all her family and friends lived, with all its comforts and privileges of concerts, church, lectures and going to a little town of not over 50 families – with about 200 army deserters, negro slaves who had run away from their masters. Think of it! What a desolate life she must have led in order that I could again have an opportunity to make good and her sons and daughters could advance to their present status of life. She started Sunday School and is now loved by all the old neighbours descendants for miles and miles in that vicinity.

We were certainly poor folks when we came west. A wife and a son and ten dollars were all my earthly possessions. Uncle Archie's fifty pounds came to us about then and it was certainly welcomed cash. Uncle Archie was my father's uncle, a professor of Latin and Greek in the University of Edinburgh, then became a preacher in the Church of Scotland. We always corresponded a great deal and had some great arguments during the war, he taking the South side. He had always been interested in me because some time about 1853 I guess, my father went to visit him in Scotland and Uncle Archie took a fancy to father's tales about me and told father that if he would make me a professional man he would leave his all to me. He died about this time and left me 50 pounds and that was a big lump just then and came in handy in those hard times.

The Panic of 1873

You remember the picture of a little sloop that hangs over the dining room sideboard? Well, there is quite a history connected with that boat. Yes, quite a history! She was all that saved us from going flat broke after the panic of '73. Her name was the *Harry Burke*. He was the editor of a newspaper, 'The Wayne County Courier' in Detroit, that had a raffle and the other papers made a big to-do about it and busted him. He liked yachting and I thought a great deal of him, a liberal, likeable fellow in his youth. That sloop took the champion flag in the races in Cleveland, July 4, 1875, and we had hoped that that performance would attract a buyer for her. It was in the middle of hard times. Our expenses had been $7,000 in 1873 for I had built a house, but the next year I cut them to $700 and the next year halved it to $350 and we could have cut it again rather than go through bankruptcy. The voyages I made trying to sell her made history. She really marks a great epoch in my life.

In 1873 we built four boats, the *Superior, Shawnee, Sandusky* and schooner *Hartford*, finishing about June 1st, and had made big money, and were worth all of $40,000 but we didn't have it in cash. We had timber, land, iron and everything but gold, so we thought from then on we would do our own promoting, instead of building boats for other fellows. We started to build a 1200 ton schooner on our own hook for ourselves or for sale, named her *Rutherford B. Hayes* after the President of the United States. Every boat we had built had been a money maker and why shouldn't this be?

We got her laid down and, of course, thought good times would continue and, when one-half in frame, were offered $45,000 for her but she was cheap at $50,000 so did not sell. The day before the Panic I could have borrowed $100,000 in Detroit but the day after not 100 cents. Nothing doing. So it took all our cash to put the boat in frame to protect her as well as we could, and we had nothing we could liquidate and no money to pay our men with. Nothing was good for anything but dollars, and we did not have them. I had spent $7,000 on a house the year before so my personal account was about flat. We had gone through Uncle Archie's 50 pounds. John F., your father, was only a baby, so to speak, only five years old. Your Uncle George often said to me that winter, 'My toes is out of my shoes and the rain gets in father,' and I said back to him just as often, 'You'll just have to stay in the house when it rains my son.'

All I could do was just feed them so you readily see how desperate we were for cash. After things got from bad to worse we started looking around to see what we could turn to money and I thought of that little yacht which I had built in '71, so I took her to Toledo, Cleveland, Port Huron and up the river, sailing her every possible place trying to attract a buyer. If we could peddle her, we could keep going somehow.

We lived on canned meat and the worst lot of scraps possible, so we didn't have anything to spend for food, but naturally, each trip, no matter how economical we were, cost us $5.00 or $10.00. The agreement with the boys was if I sold her they were crew and would get paid and I did not, they were only out on a joy ride.

My partner, a peculiar old Scotchman, would always thunder away at me on my returns – 'Hum! Hum! Damnable thing! Another $10.00 gone! That boat will be the ruination of us yet.'
Now I was living on cats and dogs and it was all I could do to keep my Scotch mouth shut when Linn would cuss me like that. But the one try left was Chicago and I was game to go on. So in spite of the cussing, I gathered a crew and sailed. We started out for Chicago with $50.00 or $100.00. Going up there I had one of the greatest experiences of my life.

I had written to vessel owners for a tow so we caught the old *Jim Chase* to Bay City and then fell in with the *John Pridgeon* and hooked on to him to Chicago. Everything went well until in the middle of Lake Michigan we struck a squall. It was my watch below. My gracious, it was terrible! The mate came and woke me and said, 'Captain, better wake up, everyone will be for himself in five minutes.' I jumped up and knew we were in for it, thunder and lightning and terrible wind – the yacht was making all kinds of motions.

My, I have never seen anything worse! I didn't think she could stand it fifteen minutes. The tow line was in a bag and we shot our boat to the lee side, but the big boat was making no headway. I tried to get up the gangway but had to cramp myself with my knees and there I sat on the steps and said, 'Am I going to Kingdom Come?' Can you imagine the state of my mind? The first question that came up was, 'Is this the end of it all? Am I prepared to meet my Creator? What a condition my business is in to leave to my wife and boys!' 'How can she educate them?' 'Why have I not more insurance?'

It was terrific the thoughts I had and I can see myself now for I sure thought it was all over. Thus my mind worked until I was almost crazy, but in about a half hour the wind calmed down, the lightning and thunder ceased, and our steamer again pushed ahead, and we had thankful hearts that we were spared, to again take up the battle of life.

Well, the next day we got to Chicago. The papers were full of wrecks and disasters of the storm. I went up to the Board of Trade and there saw John Pindiville, who had been our agent and every day we made up parties and would go out for a sail. Everyone would bring his own bottle of whiskey and a box of cigars, but never any food. After an hour they would say, 'Captain, got anything to eat aboard?' And then they'd eat me out of house and home and leave nothing but empty bottles and cigar boxes for my trouble and expense.

I fooled around a couple of weeks talking the wonders of my sloop and advertising the big boat on the stock. Pretty soon I got down to last $10.00 bill so I sauntered up town pretty disgusted to see what boat I could tow out with and the captain of the steamer, 'Inter-Ocean' said, 'You be off the pier at 10 o'clock tomorrow and we'll throw you a line.' I told Ben Alford to see about the grub. So Alford went and asked the cook if we had grub enough to last us, and he said, 'With good luck we have, but if we are cast adrift and have to sail we haven't.' So I gave Alford my $10.00 and told him to go and get some food.

I sat in the cockpit that afternoon saying how unlucky I was and imaging what my partner would say, when along came Alford with an express wagon and commenced to pull out the grub, and thinking of the loss of my $10.00, I said to him, 'Ben, did you have any money left or did you have enough to pay for all that?' and he said, 'It cost $9.50 sir.' 'Well,' I said, 'I would go get a bottle of whiskey for fear somebody might get cold or something.' He said, 'Captain, you thought just as I did,' and pulled a flask of whiskey out of his hip pocket. And as far as I know there was not one cent on board that boat starting on our homeward journey.

The steamer took our tow line, and we lashed our tiller amid-ship and had perfect weather and four meals a day thinking of today, letting tomorrow take care of itself. Well, in four days and at about three p.m. we cast our tow line and went down the west channel to Gibraltar. We waved our farewells, hoisted the canvas, sailed towards home, and the big boat went on her way. We were making good time but the sun was too high to suit me so I hollered, 'Reef the sail boys, I don't want to get there till dark. We can all slip home, have a good sleep and take our cussing in the morning'.

We docked about midnight and I slipped up so I wouldn't see my partner till morning. I says to myself, 'How am I going to fix it up with Robert?' But soon I figured that if I could only meet my partner in the presence of men, he would not dare to cuss me, because he knew I would fight. I was Scotch and did not take his loud mouth in the presence of men or other people. Then I had an idea! I waited until he was busy opening the mail because he was postmaster in our little town. I would just appear before him while he was opening the mail bags. He always opened them at a certain time and there was always a crowd around, for everyone came with the expectancy of receiving a letter whether they had ever received one on their lives or not.

When the stage was set I made my appearance and was greeted by a rough, 'Hum! Hum! Got back ain't you? Didn't sell the boat, did you?' I was preparing myself for the worst, for if history repeated itself I would hear no words of praise for my honest though futile endeavour. But the fates were kind, and at the psychological moment, as we would say now, a boy came in calling for a Mr. Craig. 'Mr Craig here? Mr Craig here?'

It was a telegram! I hurriedly opened it and it said a Mr W. W. Bates was coming to look at the hull and if all was as I had represented, no doubt his principal, Mr W. T. Baker would buy her.

So that afternoon Bates, who afterwards became Commissioner of Navigation of the United States, came and inspected the hull. He took an adz and went all over it, chipping here and there to see if he could find any place where there was rotten wood. I think I sent George (then about nine years old) after that adz. He went a-flying for he was as interested as I – though for a very different reason – to get rid of that old hull. I was thinking only of cash, while he could see the end of a disagreeable daily chore; for after school each day he had to take a sprinkling can of water and help salt the frame to preserve the wood so it wouldn't rot.

Bates asked conditions in the contract that we wouldn't stand so he went back to Chicago. In a day, however, we had another wire and a contract to deliver the *Hayes* by the first of October. So we were saved from bankruptcy because that little sloop had carried me to Chicago, and by Thanksgiving time we had about ten or fifteen thousand dollars left after all debts were paid.

This is one of the episodes of my life that caused me to think-think-think and I resolved and determined I would never be in debt again. Of course I borrowed from the bank to carry on legitimate business, but I resolved never to buy anything as an investment if I had not the money to pay for it, and I never did – and being in that condition was in a position to come to the help of my boys, when they, from inexperience, were in somewhat the same condition as I had been in 1873.

Right here, while talking of sailing, my memory goes back and I recall very well an instance that happened when your father was a baby. Old Dr Reed said Annie (that's your Grandmother here) should have some citrate of magnesia, so I went to Trenton to get it but there was none to be had in that small town, so old Ben Alford and I took the yacht (a 20-foot sloop) and sailed to Detroit. I wanted some sash and doors and plaster for my new house and he was rigging up a sulky and had a long list of stuff he wanted so we shopped around and collected our wants, and started a nice sail back.

It was a squally day and I had dropped and hoisted the sails till I was tired of hauling them up and down, so when Ben says to me, 'John, here comes another squall, shall we try and weather it?' I looked at it and said, 'Yes, Ben, let's come about.' I had hardly said it when I looked up to watch the sails take the wind and saw the boom laying straight along the mast and knew we were going over. I went one way and she went the other and I got hold of the centreboard before she went down.

There I sat straddling the keel. 'Ben, where are you?' I hollered, and he said, 'Here I am,' and I said, 'How did you get there?' 'When I saw she was going over I slipped over the stern' he said. So he came around and I put my foot down and he pulled himself up on the bottom of the boat opposite me by pulling on my leg and he was saying, 'What a nice little yarn this will be – us two shipbuilders turning this boat over in the middle of the afternoon,' and he laughed. Just then a flash of lightning and a peal of thunder came and I thought I was thunderstruck for sure. It felt as though every bone in my back had been smashed down flat to that boat. But I straightened up and found my bones were all there and looked at Ben. He was as white as a sheet and I said, 'Say Ben, are you struck?' He said, 'No, why?' and I said, 'You are awful white.' 'Well, I must be damn white if I am any whiter than you are,' he replied.

So we pulled the centreboard up and then jumped on the side and that made the boat lay on her side and finally come up and we let the ropes go and lowered sails with her lying flat on the water. We then took some boards I had for base boards, and made them fast at the foot of the mast, climbed out on the boards and finally pulled the boat on the even keel. But we were nearly as bad off as before because the sheer of the deck made ten inches of water amid-ship. We were drifting down stream so we hollered and yelled and a fellow came along and towed us to shore on Fighting Isle. We bailed her and got the water out by our pump – but we had trouble with that pump because I had bought a bale of hair to mix with the plaster for my new house, and every so often we had to clean hair out of the old pump.

We got home at midnight and told Mamma I had the citrate of magnesia I had gone for – gave her a dose, took off my clothes, said it had rained and wouldn't go to bed until I dried out, so put some night clothes on, rolled in a blanket, lay on the floor and went to sleep.

We hadn't lost a single thing, neither door sash, blinds, or the hair that had bothered us so. Of course I wouldn't tell Mamma then because she was sick and it would have worried her and she wouldn't have slept the rest of the night. After all we had had a pleasant time but had got pretty wet.

Early Lake Traffic

Often when sitting here looking out of my office window watching those huge freighters loading and unloading their 14,000 ton cargoes in a day and realising they will clear the lighthouse before I get back here tomorrow I think of shipping as it was in 1866 when I came West. Then most of the vessels of the lakes were canal schooners, carrying 500 tons of ore or coal, or 16,000 bushels of grain, so as to carry cargo for two canal boats of the Erie Canal. Package freight and passenger steamers were about 150 feet on length and most of them were high pressure. Wood was fuel as coal was expensive and burns out boilers in two or three years. These schooners would take most of a week to unload, and were towed through the rivers by large tugs.

The old schooners would make about six or seven trips per season from the head of the lakes, or Chicago or Buffalo. Lumber and grain were mostly the cargoes carried. If I remember right, 100,000 tons of ore were carried to Lake Erie ports in 1866 and freights were as high as $3 per ton, and I have seen wheat freight as high as 19 cents per bushel. In 1867 the schooner *James F. Joy* was built to carry 1200 tons and it was considered wild and an extraordinary boat. It was thought that with a few such boats that all of the grain and lumber would be carried in half of the season.

The same kinds of improvements have been made in loading and unloading coal and ore. Loading coal is from cars to ships now, at the rate of a carload of 75 tons in one-and-a-half minutes. And they can unload ore at the rate of 40 tons per minute with five unloading machines.

At the time I speak of, in the sixties, I do not think there were over 100 men in the United States who could lay down and draft a ship scientifically. In fact, ship building was an art and not a science. A builder built a ship just a little longer and a little more beam than his last one and see if she was strong enough to carry her load – and thus the merchant marine of the lakes finally came up to steamers of the present capacity, carrying 14,000 tone of ore and up to 400,000 bushels of grain.

Up to 1876 the draft was governed by the water at Lime Kilne Crossing, which was thirteen feet. This has been gradually increased to a draft of nineteen feet, ordinary weather. Our facilities for handling ore and coal has been so improved that it is now nothing uncommon for a steamer to come into Cleveland or Conneat or Ashtabula at 6a.m., unload 12,000 tons of ore, load 12,000 tons of coal and be out of port before sunset.

The merchant marine of the lakes has become a science and in fact is now only a ferry – the large steamers of the ore companies making a regular trip a week. Many of them make thirty and thirty-five cargoes per season which lasts about seven and one-half months, as navigation usually opens May 15th and closes November 30th. The old wooden steamers are almost all gone and also wooden ship builders. In fact today there is only one builder alive, who was building ships in 1866; that is James Davidson of Bay City.

But great improvements have been made, for instance, we had no car-ferries to carry cars over rough waters in those days. In 1892 we were asked if it were possible to build a ferry to carry cars across Lake Michigan, sixty miles across and 500 feet deep. Building those ferries was one of the hardest jobs we ever tackled. The building of car-ferries was a new departure in shipbuilding – at that time the only smooth water car-ferries were those carrying cars from Canada to the United States across the Detroit and St. Clair rivers, while across the Straits of Mackinac was the only place where there was open water to navigate. And even those were not built with the idea of rough sailing but to navigate through the ice in winter time, keeping the Michigan Central Railroad open between the northern and southern peninsulas of the State of Michigan.

The question of building car-ferries to connect the Ann-Arbor railroad with the railroads of the west side of Lake Michigan was a new proposition entirely. The ferries crossing the Straits of Mackinac took cars on over the bow and discharged them from the bow. We had made all sorts of drawings according to the only known scheme with the bow open, but were not satisfied that ships built in that fashion would be able to navigate rough waters. Suddenly my son George conceived the idea of having the bow closed and the stern open to load and discharge the cars over, and he so successfully evolved plans along this line that since then every car-ferry made has been built along the lines of the first Ann-Arbor car-ferry.

Well, we finally made a contract to build two boats of this new design which would carry cars but had to wait for a competent navigator to say they were as safe as any boat on the lake. They behaved perfectly - though *Ann-Arbor Number One* and *Ann-Arbor Number Two* had to carry cars for three years before they were pronounced a success by the sceptics. Now over thirty ferries are almost as regular in trips as railroad trains.

Passenger steamers by viscous legislation have almost been driven from the lakes. In my recollection we had ten passenger steamers going and coming out of Toledo every day, and doing a profitable business, and most of the other ports of the lakes the same, and now passenger business is only carried on package freight boats carrying railroad freight and this without benefit to anyone so far as we can see. All this as the result of the extra expense caused by increasing the number of men to navigate steamers which marine men think are superfluous, and all caused by the legislation in Washington that the labor organisations through the politicians have succeeded in getting passed. Toledo today has just one passenger steamer and it is an excursion boat, for people will get hungry for a ride on the water. It is just terrible when you think of it – everything going into the construction or fit out of a ship, then we pay taxes and when she is completed she has to compete in the *markets of the world* for work, when other countries' competitive cost is sixty per cent of ours.

The cost of construction from the shovel which digs the ore or coal, the railroad which transports it, the furnace and rolling mills which make it into plates and shapes, the workmen who fabricate it into ships, averages from twenty to fifty per cent above foreign workmen. All this taxation, machinery and outfitting are contributing to the support of our Government, and then when the ship is launched and completed she has to enter competition with foreign ships built at an approximate cost of sixty per cent of our ships. After they are built they must be manned with crews whose wages are forty per cent higher than our competitors on the high seas. And we are a maritime nation with over 12,000 miles of sea coast and our country is inhabited with natural seamen, who have shown their ability as seamen and shipbuilders.

Thousands of times I get out of all patience when talking of subvention subsidy to help us to do our own work. There was a time even in my recollection when the slogan was 'Free trade and sailor's rights,' but no we, on account of immigration, have developed a manufacturing nation and what would you think of the brains of a businessman, who would hire a *competitor* to deliver goods of his own make? How long do you think it would be before his competitor would have all his customers? And yet by the fear of the word *subsidy* we kill employment of over 200,000 men.

I can remember the time when foreign railroad steel was $140.00 per ton, and we by competition amongst ourselves have reduced the rail steel to $14.00 per ton at the mill. Ann Arbor railroad, from Toledo to Ann Arbor was re-railed at that price. Andrew Carnegie offered about 1900 to contract with any responsible parties who would erect a modern ship-building plant in New York, to deliver 20,000 tons a year for 20 years, of plates and shapes for $25.00 per ton. I say make conditions as they were. We now have plenty of men who would avail themselves of an offer like that and I prophesy that the natural get-up-and-get of our people is such that within ten or fifteen years of *National* competition amongst ourselves we would again be building ships for the markets of the world.

Squaring Away

After we had built several boats under the firm name of LINN & CRAIG, and my boys were beginning to grow up I decided I wanted to quit Mr Linn and in order to have all the financial backing I could, I wrote and asked my father-in-law if he had a thousand or fifteen-hundred he could lend me. Father Losee was still in New York in a sort of transfer business. He had contracts with the largest coffee, tea and spice firms in the United States to do all their carting from vessels to warehouses etc.

He had no money in the tea company, just owned the horses, trucks etc. and ran the trucking company. He was a fine looking man, a good half-head taller than I. He was one of the purest men I ever knew in my life. Instead of answering me, for we were waiting anxiously for a reply, he came to visit us that summer and he said, 'John, you asked me for money, what do you want with it?' I said, 'Life is unbearable, partner unbearable and is spoiling my disposition and I want to be in a place to buy or sell.' Also I told him that Grandma and Mrs Linn didn't get along - as Grandma wanted to run the Sunday School and Mrs Linn wanted to be Queen if that, and the whole town and she was jealous that I was getting to be head of the firm. Then Father Losee asked how the firm was situated, what we had, what we owed, how we could divide, and I told him that was what I didn't know anything about, and that was why I wanted money on tap.

I asked him what he thought and he said, 'John, I can hardly endorse it. I don't think you are doing as you'd want to be done by. How do you think Mr Linn is situated?' I said I didn't know or care; that was none of my business. And he said, 'If you and I belonged to a company that was working for a master would you say that master was doing just right to upset a business and throw everybody out of work?' and I said, 'No.' He said that was what I'd be doing. Then I wanted to know if he thought it was right for me and my wife to live in that unhappy condition and he said, 'No, John, but I'd go to Linn and say to him that I didn't want us to go in debt in any way until we had all bills paid so we'd know just where we are. Then when the debts are paid I'd say to him, I want a fair division of the partnership.'

I took his advice and kept mum until our debts were paid and we had $25,000 in cash aside from property. I then told him I was going to dissolve the partnership, divide the property and he could continue the firm or take the cash. I wanted my cash and the entire dissolution of our business relations.

We dissolved the partnership and that summer before we moved to Toledo I went to Scotland and England and all through the principal shipyards of the British Isles, getting ideas on machinery and equipment for building steel boats. It was then that I talked on the docks to the fishermen of Eyemouth and argued with them against their system of Free Trade. I told them so much that they often said, 'Would ye give us a job if we came over there, Mr Craig?' And I said 'Yes, of course, if I had one to give to you.'

I didn't see James Lough that trip for he was off to Scarborough fishing. But I told Maggie (Purves), his wife, who was my second cousin, that if he wanted to come with John and Willie (Purves), I'd do the same for him as I'd do by them. It was about six months after I said that and I had forgotten all about it, that all three Scotchmen landed in Trenton. That night in my house in Trenton I said to the boys, 'You boys have come here to get a few dollars, didn't you? But you won't find them on the streets in America, you'll find them on the trees.'

They pondered a moment and then James' face lighted and he said, 'Oh, I see what ye mean, Mr Craig, ye mean we'll have t' reach for them!' and I said, 'Yes, Jim, that's right.'

We packed them away in a boarding house and that night I said to Annie, 'They'll not all stay. I'll wager you that.' However, only John went back. Willie and James stayed and went to Toledo with us. That was all about a week before the Johnstown flood. The rain that caused the flood started in soon after these Scotchmen landed.

We stayed in Gibraltar till 1882, then moved to Trenton, Michigan, to enlarge the yard, and stayed there till 1887, when we bought the yard here in Toledo so we could handle steel plates and moved in 1888. (You see John F., your father, and his sisters Kate and Mame, were all born in Gibraltar.)

After the yard was well established in Toledo we were making good money and our family was grown up, my boys were in business with me, so I left them in charge of things and your grandmother and I took our first long trip abroad through Egypt, the Holy Lands, Europe and the British Isles.

I tell you, travel was not so common in those days as now and was considered quite an adventure.

That was in 1904 and if you will open that bookcase nearest the hall door and hand me that big notebook I will read you some of my letters of that trip if you would like to hear them.

Foreign Letters

John Craig and Annie Losee made that foreign trip, living a life of luxury and travel for several months in 1904. Their adventure took them across the Atlantic, through the Mediterranean and on to Egypt and Palestine. Then back home via Italy, France and Britain.

The letters illustrate John Craig's interest in ships and in engineering: hardly an entry passes without some reference to the size, shape, nature or composition of the vessel they were then travelling in or the ruin or artefact they had visited. For the benefit of his relatives in America, John also makes interesting comparisons with the towns and cities, rivers and harbours, monuments or people that they would have been familiar with. Towards the end of the trip John is clearly bored with yet more temples and churches and archaeology.

He is at times exasperated by the natives, and he makes this clear in language which the modern reader may find uncomfortable. His assessment of the fervour of Islamic religious fanaticism and what it might lead to is prescient. John was, after all, writing more than forty years before the establishment of the state of Israel, and a century before the emergence of Al Qaeda inspired terrorism.

At the end of their lengthy holiday John Craig and Annie Losee visit Scotland and stay with James Lough and Maggie Purves. Unfortunately there is no 'letter' which details their visit or their opinion on how Eyemouth contrasts with the Holy Land. It is likely that John decided against writing home from Berwickshire on the basis that he and his wife would probably be back in the United States before any such letter arrived. Stories of their time in Eyemouth have been handed down in an oral tradition however – along with details of some of the entries which follow.

Steamer 'Princess Irene'

January 23rd, 1904

Well we had our first meal and Mama thought she would try and eat some, so we went in to lunch and she did justice to it. Your humble servant was not afraid, so we had a nice meal.

After lunch Mama went down to our room to fix up for the trip, and it was not long before she felt like lying down, so I opened up the bag to get the medicines for seasickness, and she took a couple of doses, and she felt provoked to think a little motion of the boat should make her feel so queer.

Our ship is only an 18 knot boat, so we were happy to pass the *Kroonland,* a good deal larger boat than us. We have about one hundred and fifty cabin passengers and appear to all be nice people, particularly the DePotter party, of which however, only seven are here, the rest to meet us at Naples and Cairo. The passengers are well divided in old, young, middle age, male and female; do not see or know of any great celebrities, two or three priests, but as yet see no professionals, as actors or doctors, but will be able to individualize more in a day or more.

The 'Princess Irene' is a fine specimen of marine architecture, only four years old and beautifully fitted and furnished, and everything is clean and orderly, no noise or confusion, and plenty of help to do the work. The sea is making from the southeast and we may some of us cast up accounts before morning, but if sleep comes as it should all will be well, so ta-ta for tonight. More anon.

Sunday has been a dreary day, a little warmer; made three hundred and three miles on our course; a good chunk of sea on. The wind took a 'leeset' and came out of the northwest. Mama not able to sit up but in the afternoon took a little nourishment. No service although we have two preachers and also a priest. A leaden sky and dirty looking night.

Monday morning and it has cleared off a little. Eight bells has sounded and we are three hundred and thirty miles further on our course, and while the sea is as bad yet the ship is easier in it. We are burning one hundred and fifty tons of coal per twenty-four hours, which is not bad for two 25 inch triples. Mama is some better. I have just got her on deck, and no doubt if she could pass a whale or two she would be all right. We are in a low latitude and we do not expect to pass any ships. The bad weather leaving and continuing until now makes it so the passengers are not fully acquainted. Well, the first bugle has sounded for lunch, giving us a half hour to get ready, when we will again fill up so as to be ready if needed to feed the finny tribe.

Well, more anon.

January 25th, 1904

This is the first sunshiny day we have had, the sea has gone down and the ladies are out in all their glory, and it is exhilarating, the air is full of ozone, and everyone is contented and happy. The boys and girls are getting acquainted and pairing off, so us old ducks are going in the shade. Well, we must not complain, for I certainly have had my share of the good things of life. Mama has again got up to her feet, and it is an awful pleasure to have someone whom you feel is yours. I think now that she has her sea legs on, from this on she will enjoy it more than she has. I think she was timid at the thought of leaving our native land and trusting ourselves on the elements.

Well, let bygones be bygones. Great to tell, this afternoon I took a king of a chill, went down to our room and had a hard fever for two or three hours, so that when dinner came at seven, I let Mama go to the first dinner she was able to go to alone. Well, she managed to go through it and it is an elaborate affair, about eight or ten courses, and you sit like a bump on a log if you can not eat and wait for the next. This is the first meal I have missed, and it would perhaps have been better if I had missed more, for with three square meals and bouillon served between breakfast and lunch, and tea between lunch and dinner, we do nothing but eat and get ready for it.

Yesterday we made 387 knots and that is within 13 knots of her best time. She is not a fast ship; called 18 knots, but makes a little better than 16 on 150 tons of coal in 24 hours. Have not as yet been in the engine room but had an invitation and will soon see what the details look like. Our captain is a man a little larger than our George and about forty years old, is frank, but with all the dignity needed. It appears to be the policy of all our hands to keep the passengers in ignorance of anything except the time made every twenty-four hours, which is posted when the captain blows the whistle for twelve noon. I have talked with him some but he evidently has little conception of the magnitude of the commerce of the lakes, not having been west except one day at Niagara.

Well I am now winded; so more anon when something occurs.

January 27th 1904

I did not write yesterday because nothing new or eventful occurred and I found myself in the role of consoler, for Mama had the dumps; she woke up thinking of home and loved ones and became so homesick I had my hands full to cheer her up, but I finally drove the blues away by reading a magazine to her in our stateroom (No. 251). My-self in mind I have enjoyed every minute but when I came aboard I ate too much and clogged my diabolical system so I had to go to removing the cause with Mulholland and Carter's Liver Pills; and by tomorrow I think victuals will taste good again. We are making from 365 to 385 knots per twenty-three and one-half hours. You understand going east we are gaining on the sun about thirty minutes a day. Yesterday was not a clear, sunshiny day and maybe that was what gave Mama the blues, and when you think of it not much wonder. It stormed when we left Toledo, stormed all the time we were in East Orange and rained for three days after we left and I think her seasickness was really more a nervous sickness.

Yesterday we had a dead sea and made more motion on the boat than any other time. Today it is a beautiful, sunshiny day, with a breeze about the speed of the ship, from the S.W. and our course is East by South so we were almost in a calm. It has been just rough enough so that we have had no concerts or dancing, but nearly everybody is acquainted with everybody else, and the young men are pairing off with the girls, and if your eyes are open you see the girls have not forgotten how to use their eyes in signals to the one that is desired.

I went all through the engine department; she has two quadruples and it is an elegant engine. They were only 2 days in New York, with no time to do any fixing up. The H.P. is the forward cylinder and the 1st intermediate the after one; the after one the second intermediate next to the H.P. and the L.P. forward of 1st intermediate. I can see no real good in this arrangement except it brings the condenser away from the end of the bed plate, and another queer thing, was both the high and 1st intermediate were piston valves, but the steam chest of the 1st intermediate was on the side of the engine making it necessary for the arm working the valve to be working on an angle to reach the links. She has 225 pounds steam and a Hodem forced draft, but it is not forced at all – could almost do without it. All the bearings are large and it is a large engine and does the work easy. Has four single-ended and two double-ended and evaporates just about one ton of water per minute; she condenses for boiler and the ship's use about five tons per day. More anon.

January 30th 1904

Well, here we are about two hundred miles from Funchal. We expect to get there at daylight tomorrow morning. It being Sunday we will not see the stores as they are on other days, but will get a general idea of its beauties and surroundings. It is famed for the hand made embroideries and fine needlework made by the natives.

This is one of the most ideal days that can be imagined; a peculiar balmy air and warm so that on deck sitting around I have not had my overcoat on. Mama is now out in her steamer chair enjoying it to the fullest extent; everybody is happy and looking forward to our going ashore tomorrow morning.

Last night we had both a dance and a concert, but the little jealousies of shipboard are like all others, and I think neither was much of a success. They were from nine to eleven, all poorly attended. I went to my bunk but I got Mama to go up to report and see how these impromptus were conducted, but by the report, both appeared to be fizzles.

We have two professors of Columbia College and one of Princeton, and while I have only been in conversation with one, unless in their particular branches they may be bright, anyone would take them for ordinary men. The smoking room is not as well patronized as I have seen before, but on the whole a well ordered ship so clean that a little dirt would look nice.

We have seen a good deal of Mr. and Mrs. Messenger and they have tried to be very pleasant and companionable. We have a Dr. and Mrs. Holmes of Detroit, and little girls who are nice people, and another Detroit couple, but the passengers come from all over, some even from Spokane.

With much love to one and all, great and small, we remain your loving father and mother.

February 1st, 1904

Half way between Funchal, Madeira Island and Gibraltar. A beautiful morning, wind S.E. and going our full gait as we want to arrive there at daylight, and having 500 tons of cargo to put on will give us good time ashore, probably five hours, but will leave Gibraltar for future scrawls and talk now of Funchal. We arrived there according to program on Sunday morning at daylight and slowly made our way to the anchorage and put down our mud hook about 7:30 and it took about an hour to go through the regulations, being visited by the revenue boat and also the quarantine boat to be sure we would not bring to them smallpox or worse. After all these preliminaries, we got into a little steam launch and strange to relate, Mama was the first woman and I the first man to set our feet on the domain of Portugal from our ship. As we approached the Island from the west in the early morning it was a sight long to be remembered. It towered above the sea over three thousand feet and nearly all of it in perpendicular rock, and a cloud was floating along about half way up and seeing it both above and below the clouds was beautiful to behold; and at Funchal the houses looked like stones dropped promiscuously here and there all over. It looked a little like Seattle. As you come closer to it the Government buildings become very prominent and after that the churches, of which we found there were fifty and the poor had to support one hundred priests – terrible to think of when you see how they had to gain their subsistence. They have quite a fort there and quite a garrison, soldiers standing at arms around the streets and officers looking after them with sentry boxes every 150 or 200 feet. This is certainly a beggar and priest-ridden community if there was one. No one is above begging any place. You hire an ox team to drive you around on runners like a French cariole, and soon the driver stops and insists that you give him a drink. Then you must drink yourself and treat any of his friends near, and by this time you will be surrounded by all kinds of old women and children, who will say to you, 'Kind, gentlemen, remember the poor and God will remember you'; If you respond they will say 'God bless you'; if you don't you will be looked upon as an ingrate, but in a little time you look at them as in business and pass them by.

They have an inclined plane cog railway to the mountain top. We took it and were followed alongside by boys and girls who threw little bouquets of flowers in the car and begged for a penny and about all the pennies in the car were thrown to them. At the summit we saw a beautiful sight. While there the steamer *Maria Theressa*, the boat we came to meet, came in and let go. It is the open sea so that no boat could stay there in a S.W. gale. Our steamer looked just grand. This place depends on vegetation and fishing for subsistence. The side of the mountain is terraced and stone walled, so that I estimate it would take at least 10,000 men five years to build them. The streets are all paved with little beach stones, and different streets different sizes, some of them no larger than a turkey egg, but none of them larger than ostrich eggs.

The sidewalks are all paved with little ones no larger than guinea hen's egg and of different colors and laid out by a scientific hand. The grapes are here grown like the vines in our back yard and under the arbors the ground is cultivated in garden truck. The soil looks as tho it might be 20 feet thick. Just think of the last day of January and tulips all out and the peach trees in bloom, me without any overcoat and the air balmy and full of ozone as it can be. Well, we sauntered around the town and it being Sunday everybody was in holiday attire and those not at work on promenade, and all the well dressed women when they passed Mama stopped and turned around to inspect her get-up, and take in their minds the pattern of her suit. The stores were almost all open, and I thought if Mayor Jones were here he would see all the blessings of a wide open town, even the Bank where you could exchange your money, if you had any, was open.

Ranged along the beach were probably 300 boats like whale boats, used for fishing, and at least half a dozen steam fishing boats or tugs; these boats were drawn up over the beach stones like those the streets were paved with. They all had bilge keels on them, so when row boats need bilge keels you may depend upon it there is some sea on.

The people are all good looking, plump and not skinny, and look as though malaria was one of the blessings they do not enjoy – but being Portuguese, the girls are all brunettes, and to make themselves pretty use the flour barrel and forget to rub it off, and their color shows through the flour.

This is quite a coaling station; three steamers were here unloading coal in barges carrying about 200 tons each, which have to be towed to the lee in S.W. storms.

Well, we finally got tired of wandering around and went down to the dock and took a whale boat rowed by two men, for a change, and got to the ship safely. And such a sight met our gaze! The deck was lined with merchants who had almost everything, silver charms, drawn-work and embroidery, bamboo chairs, wine, photos, knit shawls and almost everything you could think of. There was also great excitement outside where probably thirty half-naked boys, some of them not so big as our John, were diving for silver; standing high as we were above them we could see them follow a dime and get it, and then into the boat again. A number climbed to our upper deck and dove off there for a quarter, fully 30 feet. Just think of it, on January 31st.

Well, all things come to an end, so with our stay here. Time was up and our crew cleared the deck of all in about ten minutes, and we were ready to go, hove short and at 12:45 broke ground and stood off to the South around the Island, took our departure and got on our course N.E. for Gibraltar; the monotony of our ship life again. More anon.

February 3rd, 1904

Here we are in the Mediterranean, having been and seen another Gibraltar, and if there are any more would like to have them trotted out at once, for we now know Gibraltar at the mouth of the Detroit River, Gibraltar in the Islands of Lake Erie, and now Gibraltar, the Commander of the Mediterranean, and the greatest of all is this one.

We expected to get there about daylight so we left a call for 5:45 but when I awoke found we were at anchor so I hurried on deck to see a heap of lights ranged in rows, one above another and a lighthouse in the east end of it. I thought it faced the Atlantic Ocean but found that we came thru a narrow strait and then turned to the north and we were in a horse-shoe, a good deal like the one at Sandy Hook. I saw the sunrise gun fired from the summit of the rock. When daylight came we found about ten steamers there and a large battle ship and quite a number of old men-of-war who's days of glory had gone by, probably fifty lighters and tenders and colliers, and such a sea – a regular tempest in a teapot.

The Officer of the Port came aboard in a launch and I thought they never would get him aboard; seas would wash her from end to end and she was standing on end and every side as fast as you could see her move. Well, we finally got him aboard, and about half hour later our tender came out and she did some tall 'sashaying' I can tell you. I looked at Mama and she looked a look of desperation, but she has lost all timidity now, and thinks she can go where anyone else has gone or can go, so when we started for the gang-plank why she was right behind and as eager to plant her foot on that rock as the greatest of us.

As usual we were in the front row and got our pick of seats. I chose one near a stanchion so she could hold on and we fully needed it for the tender was in all kinds of shapes in a jiffy. Oh! How they take us for tenderfeet; a fellow very friendly said he would furnish us a good carriage for four, (Mr. and Mrs. Messenger and ourselves) for $5.00. I told him that was very reasonable but would think it over. Well, the Cook tourist man came along and said they have only one price, which was $2.00, so my friend got left.

After being knocked about for three-quarters of an hour, we put our shoes on the rock, took our carriage and amidst pouring rain attempted to see the sights. We first drove up the rock, through the city to the gate of the citadel, and from there we had to walk. Well, it would have done you good to have seen your maternal parent trudging up the ascent and through the galleries which are nothing but tunnels cut through the solid rock, with here and there a gun port. Some of these ports were cut as far back as 1785. Well, after about a dozen of these Mama kicked, so I found a dry place for her and with another lady she stayed, while I followed the party until I got tired of it and came back. The citadel was still about 300 feet about us and it was raining hard. I thought I would believe what they said about it, that it fully commanded the entrance or exit from the Mediterranean. Certainly, they could sink all the ships of the world, if they were brought within range.

The rock on the west and north side is almost perpendicular and sloped both to the east and south, and it is connected to the mainland by a narrow neck of land – this is neutral ground and belongs to nobody. After registering our names as visitors we again took a carriage and went to Europa Point; this is where Gibraltar leaves and nobody takes hold, and on the way passed the most beautiful gardens (The Alameda), lilies every-where in full bloom, roses and pansies, and every variety of flowers, a good number of monuments to perpetuate the memories of England's great men, such as Nelson and Wellington. The streets of the city proper are very narrow so that two carriages could not pass, one having to wait in a recess. And of course the houses and rooms and stores are small and can not be enlarged. We were in the best bazaar and it was not more than 12 x 20 but full to overflowing with all kinds of bric-a-brac, drawn work, etc.

We then went to look over the new dry dock they were building, and it made us open our eyes. It is about half done. They commenced by cutting the steps all around and then blasting out a piece; they are now down about twenty feet, and the center will be removed as soon as they get the required depth. They tell me 10,000 men are now working at it and it will be two years before it is finished. They have a big travelling crane going on rails across it entirely and that removes the cut out stone to a train of cars which dumps it into the sea and makes a little new land.

Soldiers here, there and everywhere, sentry boxes as though you were under martial law and an enemy close at hand. To us it looked like such foolishness in time of profound peace, but I suppose the dignity of a great nation must be upheld, even if the poor have nothing to eat. No beggars here, so different from Funchal, and we saw an Episcopal church, also a Methodist one with an Epworth League attachment.

Well, it is now time to go aboard and we are tired of riding and paddling through rain and slopes, and we started down to our tender when we were astonished to find the sea all gone and the water as smooth as glass. We find ourselves aboard the good ship *Princess Irene,* she having stowed four lighters of about 25tons capacity. It stopped raining and the sea began to make, so in two hours we had to stop unloading, for the little lighter could not lay alongside. We had three large casks of tobacco roll into the sea, and five cases were dumped overboard and our captain was mad all through to think of being here all day and nothing accomplished – so he blew the whistle for the tender and we pulled up mud hooks just about sunset and skipped for Naples, taking our freight with us. More anon. Love to all.

Steamer *Memphis,* Feb. 12, 1904
In the middle of the Mediterranean

Dear Ones, One and All:
On Wednesday, the 10th, after lunch we took carriage for this steamer and without any great accident arrived about 3 p.m. and found our room

located on the main deck, about midships. For fear we would get thirsty and have only bad water to drink we bought thirty-six kid glove oranges for a livre, which is equal to twenty cents of our money. The cargo kept coming so we did not get our hatches on until after 5 p.m. and then had to wait for the mail and it was good and dark before we got off. We had some little fun with the peddlers. One of them had a little thing Mama took a fancy to and he wanted fifteen livre for it, which is equal to $3 our money. Well, we dickered for quite awhile and I finally offered him two livre, equal to forty cents, and of course he was disgusted. He then brought out another little ornament which he wanted $3 for and then another for the same money, so I offered him five livre, which is equal to $1 for what he wanted $9 for, and strange to say before we left he came and took it and I was then afraid I was stuck or thought he must have stolen them.

We weighed anchor and got underway when we were half done with dinner, and as soon as we got out of the harbour most of the ladies had business elsewhere and I got Mama in our room to bed as soon as possible, but few of the ladies slept much that night.

At daylight I turned out on the hopes of seeing Stromboli, which always smokes, but just now is not very active. However we had passed it and we were entering the Straits of Messina, which separates Sicily from Italy. It is something like the entrance to New York via Long Island Sound. The sea soon became smooth and it was a beautiful sight entering the harbour of Messina, which is like a horseshoe, about five miles long and three miles wide. About twenty-five steamers were there and probably thirty feluccas and boats without number.

After a lunch we all, Mama included, went on shore and found a town of about eighty thousand people. Took carriage and drove all over the city, stopping at all the places of interest, at the cathedral, which dates back to the fourth century, but rebuilt by Gregory, the eighth Pope. Drove up to an ancient monastery where four hundred monks and two hundred nuns used to reside, but under the new order of things viz: the separation of church and state, could not be supported and had to be abandoned, but the decorations can hardly be described, wonderful in their beauty and in the highest style of art. Mosaic work composed of pieces not over half an inch in size and yet the most beautiful pictures you can imagine, and that over a surface much larger than Memorial Hall. The main part of the city is comparatively modern, good streets and stores full of elegant things and the people well dressed and bright, and near so many beggars as at Naples. It was a beautiful day and after about four hours sightseeing we returned to the 'Memphis', where we were serenaded by a boat full of large boys and girls playing guitars, mandolins and tambourines, and the girls dancing all they could in a space four or five feet square.

About 2 p.m. we again got up our mud hook and started for Alexandria, down through the straits about thirty miles long, with a good view of both sides in smooth water, seeing Mount Aetna smoking. We soon bade adieu to the toe of the boot of Italy and took our departure. Last night was a quiet night and this morning just such a day as we often have on the Lakes. The wind was light from the S.W. and our course E.S.E. and a blue sky with a cloud about as big as a man's hand, and as it came up the wind came also so that by noon it was blowing twenty-five miles per hour, and a regular summer cobble sea, but now it is going down and I think sunset will be all gone.

This ship, the *Memphis*, is about like the *Buckman*, only twenty-five to fifty feet larger and sharper, with I should think about the same power which drives her to over 14 knots, as we went 305 knots in twenty-one and a half hours. She is easy in a sea-way with it on the quarter, but at beam I think she would roll to keeps.

At Messina I saw a little incident which shows human nature is the same the world over. After we came to anchor and the Doctor came aboard the third-class passengers stood around the gangway to get off, and at the gangway the boats were at least ten deep waiting for fares. A boat containing three women and a boatman came up on the outside, one of the women looking up on deck, gave a scream and regardless of danger jumped from one boat to another until she reached the gangway and up on deck on a run. She put her arms around a man and they kissed in the mouth and cheek and forehead and hugged and with sparkling eyes regarded each other with all the love the happy reunion gave them. When they got to the boat they were received warmly as brothers and sisters meet, but not like the previous scene.

Well, this afternoon is an awful sleepy day; we can hardly keep our eyes open. We certainly have enough to eat, coffee or tea and toast at eight, breakfast at ten, of about four courses, cold lunch and tea or wine at one o'clock, dinner at six and supper at nine. Dinner is the meal of the day, six courses with fruit and nuts to top it off with. I will finish this tomorrow for we will not get to our destination until Sunday morning.

We have had a beautiful sunrise and I was up to see it. There was a bank of clouds in the east and as the sun broke through the rifts and the golden spires and domes, and the halo all around the clouds has to be seen to be appreciated. Here we are, water, water, and I was just thinking we were going to see ruins of ages ago, but looking out on the sea can hardly realise that it has been just as it is ever since the command of the great I Am, 'Let the waters separate' and there was dry land.

We had not seen a sail for forty hours when we saw three white Russian Torpedo boats which our Captain said were on the way to Malta, where there is a Jap Merchantman which they want to capture {this was during the Russian-Japanese war}. We have just passed a German Battleship bound west with four stacks, about five miles off and must be at least four hundred feet long. We now have eighteen of our party with us and four join us at Alexandria, and all are very congenial, but a queer lot in one respect, as we are the only married couple in the party. We have old bachelors and five misses, some of which are quite antiquated, and the rest are husbands without their wives or wives without their husbands, or widows; only five men, not counting our conductors, and eleven women. There is also a party on board conducted by Bartlett, going to nearly the same places. Not many second class or steerage passengers on board, but about thirty mules. The ship is clean and quiet; do not see any officers or hear any orders, so much so you would almost think the ship was run automatically. Mama is enjoying every minute and now having her sea legs on, I will soon be able to ship her as an able seaman, with ability to reef, set, and steer.

Everything going right we will land in Alexandria tomorrow morning at about eight o'clock, and on Monday continue our trip to Cairo and then up the Nile. This is to be continued from time to time and hope you all enjoy reading or trying to read this hen scratching as I enjoy writing it. No mater where you go or what you see we do not, or will not forget those left behind, for as we look on those we meet and see, we often think, does anyone love them and have they happy and contented homes?

Well, we hope to hear from you in some shape tomorrow. With love to all, we remain,

February 14, 1904

We arrived on Sunday morning about 3 a.m. and cast anchor in Alexandria Bay to await daylight. I got on deck about 5:30 and saw the Pilot come on board and had a good view of the Bay and entrance to the harbor. It is in the form of a U – with a range of lighthouses to guide you in, and they are needed, for the rocks on each side of the channel. You can see the sea break over them. After you get within half a mile of the U a breakwater shows up and we go under it and into the harbour proper where were anchored some 60 to 75 brigs and barkentines of about three to four hundred tons burden. Then, in the inner harbour were some 25 to 30 steamers like the *Mae* or larger, unloading coal with a boom hoist, a good navy yard and large floating dry dock some 600 feet long and I should think capable of taking out the largest battleships.

Well, we went on to a dock and landed about 8 a.m. and then our conductor, Mr Potter, had a time getting our baggage in without examination, which he did by 'backshief' or bribing. He would not tell us how much it cost him. About ten we got to our hotel, the New Kedivcalle, and found it wonderful in some respects, for instance, the stairway is of the finest Parisian marble, and the marble alone cost over $100,000.00 We had a beautiful room, but the rooms to us all lack fire. The house is built of stone and unless in very dry weather makes the house feel damp. It rained all morning so we were kept in, but in the afternoon drove about the city and out to Pompey's Pillar, a shaft some 90 feet high and about 30 feet square at the base. Also the Baths of Cleopatra, which are now in ruins, but the old part of the city is very oriental.

This city was founded by Alexander the Great some three hundred years before Christ. He came over and conquered the Egyptians and believing it was the proper place to found a maritime city, to be able to make it a base of supplies in any wars he might have with Greece or Rome, made a harbor. Here it was in 1809 that Napoleon Bonaparte, after conquering Egypt, made the memorable speech to the 15,000 of his troops who remained of the 40,000 he brought with him, when he said, 'Comrades, the spirits of the heroic dead of those who lived seventy centuries look down upon us'.

Well, we visited a canal built to connect the Nile with Alexandria and a dirty ditch it is to think of using the water to drink. Here we first saw the buffaloes and camels and donkeys and jacks. We visited a beautiful garden and saw what the soil would bring forth if supplied with water. It was a sight to see the boat coming from Cairo loaded with cotton and lumber and livestock. This city had about 450,000 people and in the new part is quite modern. Well, night came upon us, and to keep warm, while all the natives were barefooted and looked as if they only had one night shirt, we crawled between the blankets and soon got warm and had a good night's sleep.

Next morning we were up in time to take a nine o'clock train for Cairo, but the road cars and everything connected with it was quite a revelation to us in railroading. The cars were about 25 to 30 feet long and divided in compartments with doors on each side and each compartment accommodated six persons, three riding backwards and three looking ahead, and alongside one side was a narrow passage-way from end to end of the car, along which the agent or, as we would say, conductor, came to see if all things were right. Well, we got started and found a good road-bed for the cars ran smoothly at about thirty-five miles per hour, and through a country hard to describe.

The land is not divided in any way tho in the highest state of cultivation, but crude. For instance, we would see a buffalo and a donkey hitched together and a steer and a mule, and a camel and a steer and any other old way, and they plowed with a stick from a tongue, the driver holding the upper end. Here the overflow of the Nile is depended on to give them the needed new soil, and so great is the deposit made from the overflow of the Nile that most of the land to the west of the city of Alexandria has been made by it, and it is said the Mediterranean actually washed the north side of Cairo some forty centuries ago.

This country between Alexandria and Cairo is cultivated by Arabs and Bedouins who actually have to build their villages every year, as the Nile washes all their huts of abode away; and a curious looking village it is. The streets are narrow and dirty and the houses are built of mud and in shape like a carboy made to carry nitro and prussic acid in. They are about twenty feet in diameter and ten feet high and the bottle necks about three to five feet higher, this being the chimney, the smoke coming out on the side of it. Just a hole to get in it, no doors or windows in it, and no furniture. When you want to go to bed just roll yourself in a blanket and lie down and go to sleep. A portion of the nomadic Arabs live in tents, for they seldom stay in a place longer than a few months; are roving something like the Gypsies in our country. We passed quite a number of towns and all were the same in general make-up.

At this season of the year, the water has to be pumped from the canal and irrigating ditches; this is done by a wheel with buckets on it and a cog wheel making a longitudinal movement, and it is turned around by a mule, or camel, or donkey, or steer, or anything at hand, and this is the present Egyptian civilization as seen by an outsider.

We saw at one place a kind of a fair and I would think two thousand of all things and kinds of humanity and animals were collected together, and all having a good time. It is hard to tell the men from the women, for the men wear a kind of pair of drawers and then over that a kind of night gown, coming down to their feet. They are all barefooted, or wear a pair of sandals, which I would not keep on my feet if I tried ever so hard. This beats Mexico for filth and misery, and yet they appear happy. The English control the country and have an Army of Occupation here, but only according to their claim to protect the Suez Canal.

Cairo has about 500,000 of which 30,000 are Europeans or foreigners. Well, we came in sight of Cairo and landed safe on time and were located in the Hotel Continental in time for lunch, and in our ride from the depot saw a cosmopolitan crowd, if there ever was one. Nubians, Syrians, Arab, Ethiopians, and original Egyptians and all the countries of Europe and America.

Well with love we remain.

February 17th, 1904

Dear Ones:

My last closed with our arrival at this hotel, and we got settled in our rooms when lunch was called.

Mama unfortunately lost one of her rubbers and we walked and finally found a place where we could get more. The reason they are not kept here is they seldom have more than two days rain a year, and of course they are not needed, but up to this time have seen nothing but rain and mud, and do not care to take risks of wet feet for her, for have been ready for any and everything and I want this to continue.

Well, on Tuesday morning we started out in carriages to see the city. We first went to the Mosque of Ali-Hassan. This was built about the fifth century and it is wonderful to see how advanced they were in architecture, for it was designed by a master mind. It is some 250 by 225 feet and had two monuments 250 feet high here. We saw the peculiarities of Mohammedan worship – while the faithful take off their shoes or sandals, we were compelled to put on our feet a canvas shoe on account of us being tourists and heathen. In the center of a large court is a great pool of water coming from a fountain; around this are seats, and we saw a man coming to prayers; he first washed his feet, then his face and then the inside of his mouth! He is then ready to pray, which he does by prostrating himself on his knees, with his face towards Mecca, and bumping his head on the ground three times, crying Alla, Alla, and that is all.

This Mosque has an inner temple where the King or Khedive came to say his prayers, and also a kind of pulpit where the priests expounded the Koran. Across the street from there, another Mosque was commenced by the mother of Hassan-Ali, but she died before it was completed, and only the tombs were completed. The grandeur of these tombs can hardly be described. The room was about 40 x 20 feet and three tombs in it of about twelve feet long and ten feet wide and fifteen feet high, and the work on them was immense; solid marble in the first place, inlaid with black walnut, ivory, ebony, solid silver and gold in all kinds of symbolic designs, representing the history and deeds of his families. From there we went to the Citadel, which commands the town. It is at present occupied by English troops, which is called an Army of Occupation, as I have said before. This is the place where the Mamelukes were finally destroyed, all except one horseman, who jumped his horse from the parapet and escaped, but the imprint of his horse is still to be seen. A magnificent Mosque was built here by the last Khedive, and he spent so much money on it that he bankrupted his treasury and was compelled to flee to Constantinople, where he died, but his body was brought back and his tomb is a magnificent piece of architecture. This Mosque was built of alabaster, which is a good deal like Mexican onyx, but not as durable, as pieces are broken off by the weather and we got a specimen, for it is the same alabaster that Mary broke the box of ointment on to our Saviour. We then went to the tombs of the royal families, and no wonder they are poor, for the cost can hardly be estimated. We saw a funeral; first three wagons with six women in each, consisting of the dead's wife, sisters, mother and other female relatives, then some mourners crying and making a great noise, then the corpse, carried on the shoulders of four men, then followed by the friends.

We also saw some ten wagon loads of women going to pray on the graves of their friends. The custom is when a woman is not used right by her husband or friends, for her to go to the grave of her father or brother and pray to him to intercede with God for her husband to improve her condition. One realises how little one really needs in this world to go along to old age, if you know nothing better, for from what we have seen so far, the clothes of the average would not bring over five cents per person, and a pig-pen with us or the meanest stable I ever saw in America would be a palace in comparison with these hovels.

Well, after lunch we again took carriages and went over to the place where Moses was found by Pharaoh's daughter in the bulrushes. Of course it looks like any other place in the neighbourhood, but one is lost in wonder and astonishment when he thinks of then and now.

We then examined a 'Nileometer'. This is a square hole made to mark the rise of the Nile, and as vegetation was dependant on its rise it was heralded from the Mosque, proclaiming the goodness of the God of the Nile in giving them the water. According to the water marks I figured about twenty feet.

We then visited the Coptic Church, noted as the place where Mary and the Holy Child stayed over night in the flight to Egypt. Then we took a drive to the University of Cairo. In it are about nine thousand students and these come from all corners of the earth, wherever the Mohammedan religion prevails, and here again you have to put on shoes for the unholy feet of an unbeliever cannot touch the Holy ground. The only study is the Koran and arithmetic, as the Koran is supposed to be the acme of all knowledge of law, science and art; and to think of it! Nine thousand students sitting on the floor with the Koran in front of them and they rocking to and fro while learning; some young and many, probably three thousand, thirty or forty years old. It is said all the wars, insurrections, and outrages committed by the Moslems, is here hatched out, and they look as though they were fit for any crime by their fanatical appearance.

After that we went through the new part of Cairo and saw much evidence of wealth, from the elegant homes of the wealthy class. We then drove to our hotel to get ready for an elaborate 7:30 dinner, and it is more trouble to get ready than I care to tell of, but when in Rome one must do as Romans do, and the women of the hotel like to parade their good clothes. Well, all things come to an end and so did the dinner. This morning we started about nine o'clock for the Pyramids and the Sphinx, and after a ride of about ten miles we stood at the foot of Cheops. Just think of this great pile of stone, covering over eleven acres of ground and more than 450 feet high, estimated to contain fully 700,000 tons of stone, some of them over 20 tons in weight! We looked up at it and thought and thought, and still had another think coming, for the magnitude of it was overpowering. It is fast going to decay. It was finished, smooth and polished granite, but time, which spares none, has laid its hand on it and its former beauty is fast disappearing.

The Sphinx is a wonderful stone – originally was some 78 feet high and 230 feet long and from ear to ear of the head some 16 feet. Alongside of it is the oldest temple known to the men of the present day. Here are some wonderful stones of solid granite – one I noticed eighteen feet long, five and one-half wide and four feet thick, and the steams and joints are wonderful to behold. In one corner I saw a stone that had the corner cut into it some three feet so as to make a bond of the corner. Some places these stones are still highly polished. A number of the party here today went to the top of the Pyramids, but I did not want to make a toil of pleasure so I contented myself by looking up to the top of it, and it was a beautiful sight, looking off twenty miles at the green vegetation on the one side and ground that will be covered with water in June, and the Desert of Sahara on the other side; sand, sand, sand as far as the eye could reach.

Well, the Arabs of this place are something great to behold. Camels without number and the most importunate men I ever saw. They could mostly speak English and were determined you must ride either a camel or a donkey, and if you do you will be charged the company's price and then you will be pestered to death for backshief or a tip, and the more you give the money the more they will bother you. Finally you give one something to get rid of him and then your trouble has only commenced for all hands will now be after you!

I think we have seen on our way to the Pyramids, at least five hundred camels, carrying almost everything in this country from cotton to grindstones. It is wonderful the loads they can carry.

Cairo, February 18th, 1904

Loved One at Home:
I think I closed my last by describing the Pyramids and Sphinx and this
morning took carriage and went to the National Museum. We drove
through the best part of the city and the most modern, past the
Khedive's palace and the barracks of the Army of Occupation, saw
the Red Coats drilling, and it was with the precision of automatons.

The Museum is a vast building of rectangular form, two stories high, a
massive structure filled with curiosities and relics of antiquity, where
everything may be seen from the mummies of Rameses II (who was
supposed to be the Pharaoh who gave the children of Israel and Moses
such trouble) to all the implements of household use and articles of
husbandry. It was wonderfully interesting to see their form of burial.

There were three classes of burial; those of the very rich, the middle
class, and those in moderate circumstances. The first costing anywhere
from three thousands dollars up, and the next costing about fourteen
hundred dollars and the next four hundred.

When a man died the high priest was sent for and an undertaking
arrived at of the cost of the funeral. When that was decided a man came
whose duty it was to draw through the nostrils with a wire hook all the
matter in the upper part of the head; then another came and made an
incision over the heart. After doing this he ran away followed by the
relatives throwing stones at him but not hurting him; after that another
came and removed the heart, liver, lungs and intestines, placing them in
four vases and sealing them. Then the body was immersed in a liquid like
strong brine for three days, after which another came and put false fold
eyes in him, painted his eyebrows and teeth and finger nails, and placed a
scarab into his heart's place and a chapter from the Book of the Dead,
like a prayer, asking this scarab to perform the duties of the heart. Then
another bound the body together with the finest linen bands about two
inches wide; but first the body was filled with spices and herbs, then it
was wound in the beautiful and symmetrical method we now see, after
which he was placed in a first coffin; on it was described all his wealth
and good qualities and then put into another coffin large enough to
receive it on which was pictured perhaps a chapter from the Book of the
Dead, prayers to assist him through purgatory and also pictures of all
kinds of food and fruits for him to eat and give any spirits he might meet

that would assist him through what we would call purgatory, to the realm of the blest. Here would also be carried the soul as it was taking its flight, assisted by the sacred bull and the sun which was the supreme god and had to be appeased, or forever after the soul would be going through space until caught by the evil one and thence destroyed, which was a calamity not to be thought of. Again he is placed in another coffin, which is pictured with the judges – I think forty-two, and a pair of scales, his heart on one side and a feather on the other, and if his heart outweighed the feather or even balanced it, he had a chance for eternal life; but if the feather outweighed his heart, evil spirits came and destroyed him entirely.

It took some thirty days to embalm and forty more to mourn before he was consigned to his tomb, which was done with great pomp, being deposited in a sarcophagus of solid granite, which before it was dug out to fit the coffin would weigh fifteen to twenty tons, and the cover accurately fitted on it with a rabbet or tongue and then sealed by the priest. Everything in connection with the burial of the dead is symbolical of some of their beliefs of the future state.

Here we saw two boats supposed to have been built over five thousand years ago, and were excavated from alongside of a tomb where they were placed to be able to carry anything needed by the soul of the dead one should they come to water – and this is Egyptian civilisation, of which I want none, for I would rather call a spade a spade, than to call it an instrument with which to make a hole in the ground.

It is impossible to describe the many interesting things seen, all money of gold and silver and copper, ornaments, and all things useful, also chariots, mummies without number representing all classes in society, the rich and middle and poor class, kings, princes, etc.

In the afternoon we rested and got a few things needed for our trip on the Nile, and saw around the city and markets and the methods of doing business, and I found a one-priced store, where I thought they wanted to deal square.

We were invited with the rest of our party to an Egyptian wedding, but were so tired did not go. It was a grand affair. First, in the afternoon a procession around the city with a band of music and the bride in a closed carriage, and the relatives in carriages following. This was a young man taking his *first* wife, but his father had twenty-two, so it will be hard to tell in a few years where this one will be – in number and power.

After a good night's rest we packed our trunk for the trip to the Nile, where we took carriage and started for our boat, the *Puritan*, about nine o'clock and we found her a good, clean, comfortable boat, much like the *Valley City*, only longer and not so much beam, as she carries no cargo, only fuel and passengers, of which our roster is some sixty-five. We had a pleasant room on the promenade deck. She is about four feet deep and is about two feet out of water, is well painted, white in colour. The river is so crooked and shallow they cannot run nights.

Well, we got off all right and after a run of about fifteen miles and lunch we made our first stop to go and see the ruins of Memphis, and here got our first donkey ride. Mama did very well for a beginner though her saddle did not fit her, but of course until she had some experience she did not know it, so we did not go all the way to the king's tombs. Went only to the city and to the images of the kings, preserved in granite, which while over five thousand years old, look as though they just came from the hand of the sculptor. The ruins were just like many we have seen, only greater in magnitude and historic interest, on account of the recent excavations and inscriptions and historical value. The explorations and discoveries only commenced in 1848 and were carefully looked after, so most things of value were taken care of and removed to the Museum at Cairo.

All things come to an end and so did our first donkey ride. I thought it not fair to snap Mama until she was more accustomed to it, and by the time we get to Judea I think she will be a star rider and be ready for anything from a lion to an elephant.

We had a good dinner and night's rest and 5 a.m. got under way for our continued journey. Today we rest but tomorrow we will ride about six miles altogether. The donkey-men are the best of beggars and expect a tip or 'backshief' and the usual price is ten cents, but it does not matter what you give them they want more, and persistent is no name for it, and the whole bank is lined with little boys and girls, some with babies in arms, begging and crying 'I am poor, give backshief.'

We are all well and enjoying every minute of the ride. Hoping this may find you all well and the damage to the yard repaired and not much in money or delay lost, we remain in love,

Dear Ones:

I think my last record took me to the night of the 20th, when we had been to Memphis. Well, we got underway again about 5 p.m. and went by pole navigation until about ten P.M. when we tied up to the bank for the night. Got under way about 5 a.m. and arrived at the village of Beni-Hassan just after lunch – 2 p.m. Got on our donkeys and lo and behold! Mama's donkey was a fast one and she started with a crowd on a fast jog – and my saddle girth broke and then one stirrup strap and then the other, so I had to get there without stirrups or girth. The route lay through a village to the tombs, and such a sight! The women were lined up on each side of the road and most of them with a baby in their hands, and it naked and generally blind in one eye and full of little sores and crying 'backshief.' You would have to see it to in any way get the impressions you receive.

Here is a country probably ten thousand years old, and from the ruins already seen must have been possessed of a civilisation somewhat equal to our own. How they could possibly degenerate is something that cannot be understood. These people, the present Arab of Egypt, cannot possibly be in any way the descendants of the dynasties of the Rameses, consisting we now know at least thirteen dynasties.

After being pestered almost beyond endurance we got to the tomb of Beni-Hassan, which is cut right into a solid rock and the room is about seventy feet long by forty feet wide, and was supported by two rows of columns about four feet in diameter, Doric in architecture except that the head was surmounted with the Lotus, which was pre-eminently the sign and command of the priest of the time and no doubt all these dynasties were dominated by them. On the walls were paintings and also the roof, telling of his greatness and also his wealth, and it is wonderful the preservation of all these paintings and inscriptions after a period of so many thousands of years; and we were also told they would have been much better and plainer only the Arabs in excavating used fire and there being no exit for the smoke, smoked them up.

I was particularly struck with the symmetry of the columns, being sixteen feet square, and each square fluted and then they had to be cut and lid out as the rock was cut out, for they were a portion of the rock itself. At the finding of the tomb, which was some fifty years ago, lots of emblems and inscriptions which were found were stolen, and what was recovered was taken to the Museum at Cairo. This tomb is up a mountain side on the east side of the river and about four hundred feet from the level of the river – and is contrary to almost all the tombs found in Egypt, for nearly all are on the west bank of the river, emblematic of the setting sun in the closing of life, and everything here seen of this ancient civilisation is emblematic of something or other and all pertaining to religion or the future state or the transit of the soul to the future state.

Here I overtook Mama and escorted her back to the boat, and on the way we met two girls about the size and age of Ruth [granddaughter Ruth Craig Merrell, then a child] and clothed in the garments of Mother Nature, and Mama took them with a snapshot, and I started to give each of them a piaster, equal to five cents and I was almost mobbed by about twenty girls, some of them, I should think, fifteen or sixteen years of age, clothed with only a rag which did not hide their sex any, and I had almost to be violent before I could get away from them, and one of them trotted alongside of my donkey for a mile pulling my hand and crying 'backshief,' but we got safely back to the *Puritan* only dusty and tired. Mama's donkeyman kept his arm around her all the time. Do not know but he was afraid she would fall, but the color of her shirtwaist certainly showed how careful he was of her at least, and I rewarded him with two piasters, equal to ten cents, and if it was not for our boatman I hardly know how I would have got out of it, for that was the usual tip, but it does not make any difference what you give them, they are not satisfied and want more. Well, anyway, Mama was troubled with a flea all night so I think she will not again try and be so gay.

We immediately started up the river and laid up to the bank about ten o'clock expecting to get Assiout right after lunch, but when we got up in the morning we were tied up to the bank and in one of the most dense fogs I ever experienced. It floated in banks and was wet as a Scotch mist. It did not lift until about ten o'clock, so we only got to Assiout at dusk and tied up for the night.

The merchants of the place came down with their goods and until the gong sounded for dinner there was bargaining for your life: I helped a lady buy a scarf. The man wanted three pounds for it; I offered him six shillings and he came down to two pounds and I went up to eight shillings and he gave it to her.

This was Washington's birthday, and at the close of dinner we had some toasts and speeches. After a good night's sleep we got breakfast at

7.30 and mounted our donkeys and before I got far I had to change mine, for I had a Jack and Mama had a Jenny and there was likely to be trouble. Although it was a dusty ride it was very interesting. We went to the top of a mountain for the view of the Nile and then to the tombs of the Wolf and there saw a cart load of mummies of foxes, for at one time they were deified. A man came around with a live hyena as a pet but we gave it a good berth, and descended again in safety.

Then we went through the city, which has some forty thousand inhabitants and is the largest town in upper Egypt except Cairo and Alexandria. This town collects the products which are principally wheat, some corn, cotton and dates. We passed through the principal street and the police had actually to force our way through the crowd doing business, and it looked as if about five dollars would buy the whole crowd.

Well, love to all and more anon.

February 27th, 1904

Loved Ones at Home:

We got under way about five o'clock and sailing all day of the 24th we arrived at Dunderah at 9 p.m., and after a quiet and peaceful night started right after breakfast for the temple of Dunderah. This is one of the greatest temples discovered; it is about two miles from the river and about three hundred feet above the river and was the site of Dunderah, an Arab village, right on top of the temple and accidentally discovered and the houses were removed from the top of the excavations to the floor of the temple, about 150 feet.

All of these temples were of the same general construction, consisting of a great court between rows of columns, generally 150 feet long, and one to two hundred wide, and the columns of gigantic size; from this court is another one in the rear called the sanctum-sanctorum in which no one was allowed to enter save the priest and king, and still another one where only the king was allowed to go. The mystery of the king was he was always considered a man of destiny, and any one raised to the dignity of king was considered to have come into this world in the same mysterious manner Christ came into the world; that his father was the sun, or if God was the moon, then he emanated from this, and thus divinity was propagated by divinity, and the recognition of it was the elevation to the kinghood, even though the king so elevated was the son of a king.

This temple is only considered second to Karnak and Luxor, which we will see on Friday. It is just wonderful to look at these great stones, some of them fifty tons in weight and yet they were transported from Assouan and taken inland and raised, and after being polished and then carved in such a wonderful manner. I estimated the carving here seen would cover a space half a mile in length and 110 feet wide and as close in figure as most of the letters we see on ads on billboards, and of the finest quality and colored so we could still see after some six thousand years how exquisitely it was decorated, and all this carving was the history of the King commencing with the deeds of his ancestors and ending with his wars, conquests and the advancement of his kingdom in science and arts and wealth.

Well, this is up to this time the greatest work of antiquity we have seen, but we are told greater is to come, but the same squalid poverty and degradation is still on every hand. It is wonderful the care of two or three kids or lambs, or a little donkey, showing that a man who owns a half dozen sheep or goats, or a couple of donkeys or a camel is considered rich, for it is no unknown sight to see quite a good sized goat or sheep carried in the arms because it may be sick or from some reason unable to walk – but go where you will and when you will, you will always see a hand stuck out to you and backshief, backshief, cried out to you. One would think they would get tired of it - for our party, I think, does not encourage it much.

We got safely back to our good ship in time for lunch and after a good deal of dickering with the merchants who brought their wares of all kinds for our inspection, and quite a good many Yankee dollars were left here, we proceeded on our way to Luxor, where we arrived at six o'clock. This is the most important town between Assiout and Assouan, where our trip ends; some 16,000 people and the site of the Temple of Karnak and Luxor.

We got on our donkeys on Friday morning and after a half-hours ride came to the greatest temple of ancient Egypt. The ruins cover 1200 acres, and it would take a book to describe it. The columns of the great court are some 90 feet high and 15 feet in diameter and built up of granite. This immense structure had a row of sphinx about 30 feet apart and nearly a mile long, and from the great hall and sanctum-sanctorum great rows dedicated to the members of the family, and for particular chapters of history here is seen on one of the walls the oldest treaty of peace on earth, giving the settlement of the war between Jereboam, King Solomon's son and Rameses the Great, also telling of the victories won by his personal courage. This had a grand road which led across the river to the tomb of the Kings, seven miles away, and once a year a grand procession was made on account of the ceremonies by the priests would take some six hours to pass a given point. Another road was made to the Temple of Luxor, which was just an annex to Karnak, and the most wonderful thing of it was some twenty or more statues of men, say about thirty feet high and perfect in proportion and detail, and while all were not perfect, yet enough of each was perfect to see exactly how magnificent they were when in their glory.

The excavations here are stopped by a Mosque of modern times, built almost in the middle of this temple and the authorities who were afraid of an insurrection were compelled to stop the explorations. Here I seen some of the most perfect obelisks in the world; on one here I could not see a blemish and its mate is now in Paris. It is thought if time and money could be obtained to excavate, that a square mile would be fully exposed of the greatest work ever performed by man. While we have higher buildings, yet nowhere on this green earth are there individual pieces of architecture so enormous in size and weight, and shows that the architecture and mechanics and even the common workman are not excelled by our present civilisation.

As I look out of this window I see some forty-five columns, about 12 feet in diameter and say forty feet from centres, the capital of the column about touching each other, and a stone reaching from centre to centre of a column nine feet square and forty feet long. It is hard to imagine how they were able to get them up there. This work is all under the government control and from the fees received are continuing the work and inducing travel here. It is estimated that 25,000 visitors come here every winter, both to see what can be seen and also on account of the dryness of the air, it curing asthma and all affections of the throat and lungs. It has two pretty good hotels here and they are full of visitors. We saw here Hall and Harry Chaney who sailed a few days before us on the *Dutchland,* and are spending six months away from home.

Yesterday morning I saw the most interesting sight since we left home. I got up early to look around and see what the place looked like and I wandered up to a Mosque and found it full of worshippers and after watching them awhile through the windows I continued on to a public square, where some six hundred to a thousand men were upon their knees in rows about six feet apart, kneeling on a piece of carpet or a handkerchief, with their shoes in front of them, and a few feet away, say ten feet, kneeling alone, was the priest. He was saying the prayer and they were responding and every once in awhile they would bump their heads on the ground in perfect unison and with military precision; a more devoted crowd I never saw. They were not looking right nor left, but with one accord attending to their devotions. After about twenty minutes of this the praying finished, the priest under a canopy of flags, commenced to read some chapters from the Koran, and the multitude stood in respectful attention, once in awhile some patriarch responding. After he was through reading, the police surrounded him and escorted him to the station house, for the populace wanted to tear the clothes from his back believing if they could get a piece of his garment it would bless them and the increase of their flocks or grain and bring good to them. They finally made a procession and under their flags went to a Mosque and continued their devotions.

To me it was a wonderful sight.

No women were at the devotions but all the little boys and girls were decorated in every conceivable way with anklets and bracelets and earrings and nose rings, some with silk and satin and barefooted at the same time. I saw large companies of women with baskets on their heads going to the cemeteries, where they pray to their dead relations to assist them in this life and let their dead relatives help themselves out of the baskets; and what is left is given to the poor on their return to their homes.

I could not help thinking as I looked into the earnest faces of those praying, that it would be little trouble to make fanatics of them who have no regard for life or anything else. We see our Nubians on the bow of our boat praying every day. They pray five times and if they commit a bad act between prayers it is forgiven at the next prayer. I found out this is their Christmas Day, being the birthday of Mohammed, and anyone going to and being in Mecca today will be saved no mater what their sins have been or may be.

Well, love to all. We are well and enjoying ourselves, but do not get many letters from home.

March 3rd, 1904

Loved Ones at Home:

Well, we were made happy by a letter from John F. and Mamie, and glad things are no worse and hope by this time things have become normal.

This is a beautiful day with thermometer about 75 degrees but cool in the shade. My last closed with an account of Karnak and Luxor. On Sunday morning we got on our donkeys and rode about three miles to see the temple of Rameseum the Great and it is like all the rest; had been dug out of a mountain of sand and like all the rest is full of carvings giving the history of his dynasty; but the greatest curiosity was his statue, which had been toppled over by an earthquake. It weighed over one thousand tons and how it was quarried eighty miles away and then brought here and erected in place is beyond my comprehension, for I have no idea how it could be done now in our time without an enormous expense of both time and money.

We got back in time for lunch but both tired and dirty, and rested all afternoon, saw the temple of Luxor by moonlight and it was full of shadows. Left about 3 a.m. Monday and put in an uneventful day, restful in the extreme. The river here is not so wide as below, but just as crooked, sometimes going southwest and then again southeast.

The green of the banks is very beautiful and it is fertile if it only gets water. In order to give it water, sometimes men with a kind of a well sweep would raise water by the bucket, say 16 feet, and it would flow to a well hole where another man would raise it another 16 feet, and it would go to a third one, and then it would be high enough to flow on the desired ground; and these stations would often for miles be not over 150 to 200 feet apart, and the men would be stark naked except a little breech cloth and it would be meagre.

We arrived at Kom Ombos just about dark and tied up for the night, and in the morning examined this temple – or the ruins of it. It was carved as fully as the rest but it was in a better state of preservation, as the colors of the paint could be examined and admired after a period of four thousand years. The carving was not in as high a style of art as Karnak or Denderah, but it shows the patience of the builders and also how the nation felt it must preserve its history, and this appears to have been the only way known to them.

We arrived at Assouan about 2 p.m. and this is the end of our journey up the Nile. It is a comparatively modern city of nine thousand people and gets its importance from the fact that a large dam was built here to control the waters of the Nile and not permit the waters to at once run off and leave the bed of the river almost bare. It has three good hotels and is the centre of a large trade which reaches almost to Khartoum in the Sudan, where the English had so much trouble with the Sudanese.

On Wednesday we visited the dam and also the Temple of Jesis, and there is now a good part of it under water, the water being over twenty feet around it and by this dam some millions of tons are stood here. Three locks with a fall of about twenty feet to each lock permit boats to go above it. The dam, I should think, is over three miles long of solid masonry, with gates to open and let as much water through as needed. It is a work a good deal like the locks at Sault Ste. Marie, built at a rapids, and I would think cost $10,000,000, at least, and the town of Assouan was partly built upon the great amount of money expended on the dam.

The Army of Occupation keeps a garrison here so no enemy can come from the Red Sea and go down the Nile to Cairo or Alexandria, and also a garrison at Cairo and Alexandria so no army can come up the river.

Here we had a sand storm while at the dam, and it is something terrible, for your eyes, nose, mouth, hair, ears and anything around you is filled full of this alkali sand, and for two days you will be washing, spitting, blowing your nose and altogether very uncomfortable.

Here are all the big quarries from which the kings got their granite to perpetuate the knowledge of their greatness. The stores here are filled with curiosities and you are apt to be cheated almost out of sight. For instance, you will ask a man what he wants for something and he will say three pounds, and before you are through with him he will sell it to you for three shillings. When you tell him the price is too much he says, 'What you give?' And you will be kind of ashamed to offer him one-tenth of what he asks. And yet then you are liable to get stuck, for he may and likely will say, 'All right, you good gentleman, you take it.' We have got a few little things here.

We saw life as it is here, and they tell us it is much improved in the last three or four years, and this morning we commenced our return trip. We expect it will be uneventful and will get back to Cairo about next Wednesday. There is much sameness here; the tombs are on the same general plan and having seen one you have really seen them all. Some go into ecstasies over the magnificent grandeur of the former civilisation, but I cannot, and look at them as any other ruins in this or any other country.

The scenery of the Nile is grand and beautiful, big mountains on every side a good deal like the Palisades on the Hudson. Sometimes the river is wide and shallow and then narrow and deep; the fertility of the soil, depending as it does on the water of the Nile, does not make a belt of much more than a mile wide which is fertile and cultivated and that only by irrigation, where they sometimes put two and three crops in per year. Most of the land is tilled on shares, the man doing the labor, which includes the irrigation, and yet sowing three bushels of barley or wheat they get about seventy in return, and most of the land is cultivated in that way; but where a man works by the day he gets, if a good man, about twenty cents. You can imagine how much he can enjoy on that, yet they appear happy, for they always laugh and sing at work, but the greatest mob you ever saw is when they are trying to get you to hire their donkeys, and they know enough English to make you laugh. This one will say, 'Good donkey, his name Jim Corbett.' Another one will be 'Yankee Doodle', and all the names they have ever heard, but I think the English language will be the tongue of this country within the next twenty-five years. We up to this time have not been where we could not find someone to talk English in a minute or so.

These vendors have an awful horror of the policeman, as he will with a cane pound right and left, but his back is no sooner turned than they are at you again, determined to make you buy their wares or ride their donkeys. These Nubians are great big strong men, not much like our negroes, and yet some of them are so very black. I think charcoal would make a white mark on them. Their features are different, not the wool on their heads, nor the big thick lips, nor the great smell our darkies have, but superstitious to an alarming degree, the kind fanatics are easily made of.

This is a wonderful climate for anyone having any bronchial trouble, for it never rains. The sunsets are wonderful to behold. The afterglow casts itself over the sand hills and makes them look almost like gold. We had one hot day when it was 93 in the shade and we could hardly realise it was March 1. The date palm is almost the only tree on the banks of the Nile and it is very profitable, bringing a good return. They grow about fifty feet high and nothing but a little tuft of palms on top, but look pleasant to the eye. Oranges are plentiful and juicy and sweet, much more so than in California, but not so large. We use them almost altogether for drink, as we dare not use the Nile water. We drink at the table a water something like appolinaris; tea is good, but we only get it for breakfast, and we would give a good deal for a little of Madison Avenue cooking for a meal or two.

Well, my budget is pretty nearly full and will close with love to all at home and hope you are all well as this leaves us at present.

March 4th, 1904.

Our Dear Children One and All:

I think my last ended with a description of Assouan and the great dam at Assouan, seven hundred miles from the Mediterranean to control the overflow or high water of the Nile so another crop can be grown. We arrived at Luxor today about 2 p.m. and visited the stores and shops and got rid of some of our loose change. Visited the American Consul and found him a colored man, but these people are not like our negroes except they are black or nearly so. I cannot describe the color, except to say black as it could be and without any shine or lustre, a dead black. They are different from our negroes in habits and nature, not lazy or indolent, but hard workers, and if they had an opportunity would excel in most kinds of work. For instance, coming downstream our boat is hard to control. As we were approaching a bridge and could not stop, and realising that the bank was lined with stone which if we touched might make a hole in our hull, three of our deckhands jumped overboard with a line and swam ashore and got a turn around a post and stopped us from crashing into the bridge. Now they had to swim fifty or seventy-five feet to do this. I thought it would be a good while before any deckhands in our country would jump over with a line to save a collision. We see men elevating water and working steady and it is very hard work, showing the difference between them and our negroes.

We stayed all night at Luxor and had a look at the ruins by moonlight. While we were again filled with the magnitude of the ruins, yet we are being filled up with them.

After an uneventful day spent looking at the varying scenery of this wonderful river we arrived at Belleanah about 5 p.m. and tied up for the night. The place, being interpreted is Anine the Belle, is quite a place of some thousands, and from here next morning on your mother's birthday started on donkeys for the Temple of Abydos some seven miles distant. The temple is somewhat different from the rest, being built broad instead of long, but the same kind of architecture and carvings. The most of the stone was of hard limestone of a very fine grain almost like alabaster, and the carvings were almost perfect and of the finest character. It is wonderful how the colorings of blue and red and yellow have stood and not faded, as this was done some 3500 years before the Christian era.

We also visited an old Coptic monastery which is now a school, and it was a wonderful building, being of about 100 feet long by 75, with three rows of columns; the roof supported by these columns was arched both ways to form an inserted half globe all of brick and of great antiquity.

This Coptic Church is a Catholic church of the Greek or Russian from the tenets of which I do not know, but exerting a great influence here in educating their children. I was more impressed with the labor and expense the Government has gone to in irrigating this country, going out seven miles, which we think is the broadest strip of country we have seen under cultivation. There were some five canals about 20 feet deep and some 30 feet wide at the bottom and 100 feet wide at the top parallel with the Nile and, we were told, some 10 miles or more long, for no other purpose than to hold water so that the people in between these canals could pump the water and irrigate the land. They are dry now as the Nile is at its low stage, but I never saw finer wheat or barley or beans anywhere.

A great many villages were seen on the way. The houses were built by sticking corn stalks into the ground and piling some mud on both sides and lacing them together at the top. They only covered over little rooms where the dwellers would sleep. As it never rains here they do not need any protection from inclement weather, and only need to keep the wind off them at night and in the early morning. A good part of their business is raising stock, sheep and goats, and they make them eat a place clean before they get a chance elsewhere. They hobble them by tying the front feet together say about six or nine inches apart and then from the middle of the string another about four feet long to a stake, and they eat every spear before they can move a foot. Little boys and girls attend them and some or them not any bigger nor older than Donald, and it is just wonderful the control they have over them.

From looking over this country you would think a man or family with

25 sheep or goats was a rich man. Nearly all the land is worked on shares and irrigating is the most labor in connection with the crop. A great many villages are quite a distance from the water and it is quite a sight to see anywhere from five to twenty women down in the water filling their water jugs, which I would think would hold about two or four pailsful, and then lifting them to their heads and perfectly balancing them. They walk in procession back to their homes – or hovels we would say. They generally take a bath while at the river and as they have nothing on but a kind of gown and a shawl for head covering, as no woman must have her face seen, it does not take long to dress or undress.

Very few horses or even mules are in the country; the beast of burden are either donkeys, camels or the buffalo, which is not like the bison of our country except in form; no shaggy mane or wild look, docile and lazy, having to be forced to work. The oxen do not grow large, but like our own plodding faithful beasts used mostly to hoist water which I think I have before explained. We have seen a good many fishermen on the banks with a pole, and see some fish caught. I think they are like our sunfish but do not think many follow fishing for an occupation.

Well, after our great ride of fourteen or fifteen miles, just you think of your mother on a donkey for four hours in the hot sun, no sunshade, and dust the last part of the way in clouds and yet today she is all right and you will know just how frisky she is getting. Her donkey and her boy kept her in employment. You may be sure I snapped her camera on her to show you how she looked on a donkey, and this morning we arrived at Assiout, where we stayed for an hour and a half to give the people time to spend their money on 'gewgaws,' and all sorts of curiosities of this country.

Jerusalem, March 15th, 1904

Dear Ones:

My last we were still on the Nile, and arrived at Cairo on Wednesday morning, March 9th, and after settling ourselves at the Hotel Continental, and reading our mail, which we thought meagre, finished our visit to the National Museum, where we looked at all the jewels, precious stones and relics excavated from the tombs and ruins we have been looking at the last twenty days, and it is wonderful how well the

Egyptians left behind them the history of their respective dynasties, in their sculpture, paintings and hieroglyphics, and how different from any other nation of either ancient or modern times, a complete history being made from that left behind, and our conductor, Dr DePotter, can read them just as readily as I can English.

Went Thursday morning to the Tombs of the Califfs, of which Cayer Bay is the finest, built in the fourteenth century, beautifully preserved and money left to keep in repair, but as with all things Turkish most of it was stolen. Here is a mark of Mohammed's foot as it was pressed in clay, and brought from Mecca for the faithful to venerate and adore. In this tomb the best specimen of Arabic stained glass work is seen, said to be unexcelled by any in the world; connected with the tomb is an altar for the descendants to worship when visiting their dead. Also visited the new Arab Museum where we saw all the relics saved from the Mosques of the Sultans, some doors carved over fifteen hundred years ago. Lamps which are worth over $1,000.00 on account of their beauty and antiquity.

Mama was not feeling too well, somewhat tired out, so she stayed in her room while I went to the market, and to my surprise I found it would compare favourably with any in our own country. Everything looked clean and I will certainly eat while in Egypt with more relish than formerly.

In the afternoon we went to a meeting of the Whirling Dervishes and had enough or we would have gone to the howling Dervishes also. These Dervishes are sects of Mohammedans who are advanced from common people by faithfulness and are all over fifty years of age. The meeting house is some seventy-five feet in diameter, octagon in shape with an outer place where anyone and even Christians can go.

About twenty men ranged themselves around the room and some high monkey-monk up-stairs reads from the Koran, and two others up-stairs with a boss director down-stairs make the responses kneeling, and at each response kiss the floor in front of them, and in about five minutes the two up-stairs commence to play on a kind of an instrument like a ten-cent whistle, and the others get up and march around the room and as they pass the high monkey-monk down stairs, they bow to him and kiss his hand. After they all went through this part twice, the tune changed just a little and then each one passed the big gun and turned around and bowed to his follower, leaving a space of about six feet between them. Then after taking two steps backward commenced to whirl around and their long skirts stuck out like an umbrella, and with arms extended, one hand the palm was turned up and the other down. This they continued until they raised such a dust that we left in short order, for the perfume in that crowded place was anything but pleasant. We could not see any reason or sense in all their actions except their sincerity, which is certainly pronounced, for they turn their heads nor eyes neither to the right or left and their faces are as long as your arm.

The women of the church were upstairs, behind some lattice work, peeping through; we could hear them but could not see them. While out this morning I met a young man who wanted to talk to improve his English; he attends a school, and from him I think I got the common custom and belief of the marriage relation. He said, when I wanted to get married I go around until I see a girl looking out of a window I think I would like to marry. I only see a little of her, so I go to her father next day and tell him I would like to marry his daughter. He wants to know how much I will pay for his daughter, and I want to know how much he will take. He finally says $1,000.00. I tell him I cannot pay that much and say I might pay $100.00, and if he is satisfied he goes to his daughter and tells her he has found a man to be her husband. She says let me see his picture, or tells me to pass his house at a certain time, when, if she is pleased, she says yes. I go to see him the next day and he still wants $1,000.00; he finally says he will come down $100 and I go $5.00 and we finally meet by he coming down $100.0 and I going up $5.00, and I pay the money and the father buys furniture with it, and that is all about it, and a man can have as many wives as he wants. When he is tired of any one of them he gives her a paper and sends her home, she taking any girls they may have, but he the boys.

Most men have but one wife now, but this one may be his tenth or twentieth, so he will tell you he only has one wife, and such a thing as a wife going off with another man is unknown, for the law would put her in prison if her husband did not take her back, and this is a religion as old as ours, and increasing at a wonderful rate.

On Saturday I took mama to the bazaars and my pocketbook looked as if an elephant had stepped on it. On Sunday morning we left Cairo for good for Port Said, and certainly Cairo is a cosmopolitan city, more so than even New York, for I think no nation under the sun is not represented here; all classes, kinds, and conditions, from Khedives, whom we saw twice, to Dukes, Counts, Princes and Princesses and even Negroes, rich, poor and the go-between; all colors, white, black, brown, yellow, and all shades between; the blackest black I ever saw, and no shine or lustre to them, and the Sudanese are all marked by cuts on their cheeks to show the tribes they belong to.

Some beautiful buildings, statues, parks, hotels and mosques, and also the greatest degradation that one can conceive of, not clothes enough to cover them and home wherever night overtakes them, and yet religious fanatics of the greatest fervency. I think, however, Cairo has a great future, for with the great tourist travel here new ideas will be coming, and with them capital, so that things will soon become different.

We arrived at Port Said before dark and found it like an American city, it having come up entirely since the opening of the Suez Canal, and destined to become the port of entry of all Egypt. The streets are wide, the houses large and modern, good docks and anchorage, and everything modern except the Arabs, who will soon be amalgamated in the progress of one or two generations.

We embarked on the good steamer *LaClare,* which means Cairo, and had a quiet night crossing this end of the Mediterranean, and arrived at Jaffa at daylight, and here we saw the methods of the Turk to collect revenue. It was two hours before the doctor would come aboard; then he had to have his breakfast and some whiskey, and then business was commenced in earnest; the passengers all were passed before him for inspection, names called out and examined, and that was quite a job, and if nothing extra had been paid him we might have been there yet. However about 10 A.M. we got all through and as soon as the doctor's flag was lowered a race commenced by the boats to get the passengers and baggage, and a good one it was.

This landing is as much feared by tourists as any, as it is on the open sea, and we go between rocks to make a landing. This is where Hirem, King of Tyre, bought the rafts of cedar for King Solomon to build his Temple.

I forgot to say incoming from Cairo to Port Said we passed through the land of Goshen where Joseph ruled and sent for his father and brethren to keep them from starving during the famine in Egypt, and now, as then, it is a beautiful fertile plain, well watered by the deltas of the Nile, as recorded in Gen. 45, 10th Verse.

Also we saw the graves of soldiers killed in taking Alexandria in 1881. We passed the customs without having our trunks opened by contribution to the frailties of the officer. We then took carriages and went to the house of Simon the Tanner, where the apostle had his dream of a sheet being let down from heaven and he was told to 'arise, slay and eat,' and the well where he drank, and the water raised just the same. It was on the roof where he had his dream, and it appears to be well authenticated.

We also went to the house or Dorcas, where the apostle raised Tabitha, her daughter, from death; also the Tomb of Dorcas, where now is a Russian Greek Church.

We had a good lunch at the hotel and took a train for Jerusalem at 1:30 P.M., passed through the plain of Sharon, also the land of the Philistines (Solomon's Songs, Chap. 2), flowing with milk and honey, (Judges, Chap. 12); also where Samson tied the foxes' tails together and by them set the Philistines on fire – at Giaza; passed the village of Lydda {Acts 9, Chap. 32}, where Peter was staying when he was sent for to raise Dorcas' daughter Tabitha. Also Bethdager, where the God of the Philistines lived.

This country could easily be taken for Ohio, the wheat and barley was so good and a nice rolling country. Also saw Ramleh, where Joseph of Arimathea came from when he went to Jerusalem. Zoras, the home of Samson; Cave of Samson, where he hid when pursued by the Philistines (122 Psalm, 'My Feet'), and at 6 p.m. we arrived in the city of David, Jerusalem, and with One of old, Mama can say, 'How I have suffered for thee,' for on the steamer it was so crowded we had to separate, and she went with two other women of our party, but at 1 a.m. fleas woke her up and she killed ever so many and had to sit up the rest of the night. If it had been rough she would have had a time; she says she will remember it to her dying day.

Well, when we got to our hotel it was something great, candles for light, two iron bedsteads worth with us about $2.50 and no carpet. We made up our minds to make the best of it, and after dinner we were both tired enough to sleep the sleep of the just and did so, and awoke refreshed and ready for another day of looking at this ancient city of David. Last night we did not go within the gates, our hotel being outside of Jaffa Gate. After breakfast we went to the Church of the Sepulchre, which was built about 336 A.D., and saw the spot where Christ's grave was located. This church now is used in different parts by all sects except Protestants, and the Turks by treaty at the end of the Crimean War were made custodians of it. Here is the slab on which the body of Christ was laid. Here was the sepulchre of Christ, the Tomb of Joseph of Arimathea, and the place where the stone was rolled away. This church has a circular dome, beautiful and magnificent with paintings and carvings, and a handsome edifice built in the center of this hall 100 feet in circumference. Over the tomb of Christ, Joseph of Arimathea and Nicodemus were buried. Assirian, Greek, Catholic, Coptic, now worship here at different altars. We also saw the spot in the garden where many met our Saviour and thought He was the gardener. We also saw the place where Christ was kept the night before the Crucifixion, also the place where the soldiers cast lots for his clothes. Also the place where Queen Helena, mother of Constantine, is reputed to have found the cross of Christ and proved it to be His cross by a child coming to life after death by being placed on it, and this is one of the great articles of faith of the Armenian Church. Saw the place where Christ was crowned with thorns, and a great deal more which I will continue in my next.

With much love to all, we remain

Jerusalem, March 19th, 1904

Our Dear Ones:
We are well but Mama is tired all out so much so that we will not do any sight-seeing for a couple of days.

I think I closed by last describing a part of the Church of the Holy Sepulchre. We saw the spot where Christ was crucified, the very spot where the cross stood, and the rent in the rocks when He gave up the Ghost. It is the belief of the Greek Church that Adam was here made of Christ and that this spot is the center of the earth. We saw the many changes, selling candles as they did in our Saviour's time. We visited the Tomb of Melchesidic, where he and Adam were buried. Also the Church of the Lutherans built by Emperor William on the site of the house of the Order of Jerusalem, Knights of St. John, where he instituted the order of Knights Templars.

Jerusalem is built on four mountains – Mount Zion, Mount Moriah, Mount Ekra and Bezeita, and it has been sacked and destroyed some four times, but little of the ancient walls of it are left, just enough to show where it was, and it is queer that the Jews left no inscriptions by which its history could be authenticated. We saw the house of Caifas, the high priest in power in Christ's time, also the place where Peter denied Christ three times when the cock crowed; saw the prison of Christ after condemnation and before the crucifixion, also the stone which was rolled away from His Tomb.

We visited Mount Zion, the city of David; saw lepers begging in front of its gates, with their fingers eaten off with leprosy. Here we saw the upper chamber where the Last Supper was eaten, and the Lord's Supper established.

The Tomb of David, which is now in the hands of Mohammedans, and Jews are not allowed to enter; they claim him as one of their first and greatest prophets. The oldest kind of a bell in the world at the entrance of St. James Church, which is a piece of metal four feet, eight inches wide and three-quarters thick; this is struck as you enter the church to let the Lord know you are there for Him to hear your prayers. Saw the place where St. James was beheaded and buried. This church belongs to the Armenians and is visited by about 60,000 pilgrims every year. Here is where the Bishop and Patriarch of this Church come every year to give their blessing to the pilgrims. It is a beautiful structure and often 10,000 pilgrims are entertained here at one time. The Greeks or Armenians never sit down in the church.

The next day we left for Jericho (March 16th). Came all around Jerusalem, from our hotel to Damascus Gate, passed Kidron of the Valley of Jehosaphat by the Mount of Olives. Saw Jews praying over the tombs of their dead by the hundreds; passed through Bethany, the apostle's fountain, the inn of the Good Samaritan, and on to old Jericho of the time of Elisha, where was his fountain and well, where he healed so many by its water, and saw the place where he was fed forty days and forty nights by the sarem, and came back to the Jericho of Herod's time.

After lunch went to the Dead Sea, and tasted its waters, which is hard to describe for when it first enters you mouth you think it is only very strong salt water, but the after-taste is bitter and so peculiarly bitter you cannot describe it, only disagreeable in the fullest sense. I washed my feet in its waters and had I thought of it would have fixed myself to bathe in it. While using, it was very refreshing but it was impossible to rub off the sticky feeling it left, and did not get rid of it until I washed it off in fresh water. It is some forty-seven miles long and five miles wide and 1300 feet below the Mediterranean, and 4,000 feet below Jerusalem.

We then went up to the River Jordan, where John Baptized Christ, and washed my hands in it. It is about 200 feet wide, muddy about like our Maumee, and a current of about one and one-half miles, but it is difficult to describe the feeling which comes to you as you look at and attempt to see in your mind's eye the scenes as portrayed in the New Testament, which here occurred two thousand years ago, and from which all the present civilization has come, for under no other religion which we have as yet seen, has such great blessings come to humanity as by the teachings of Christ.

We also saw Gilgal, the place where the children of Israel took from the Jordan and erected 12 stones for the 12 tribes of Israel, and where they received no more manna as they were about to enter the land of Canaan.

We stayed all night at this historic place of Jericho and in the morning commenced our journey back to Jerusalem, an ascent of some 4,000 feet, and some eighteen miles. We stopped for an hour at the house of the Good Samaritan and also the apostle fountain, and certainly this is the wilderness of Judea, for nothing grows, but stones big and little, and I think we only saw one bird all the way, but pilgrims by the hundreds, and we were told some of them came 2,000 miles to be here for Easter, most of them over 50 years and a good many 75, and all walking with a pack on their back, and they have been saving all their money, for some of them twenty years, for this the greatest feat of their lives. We saw many of them prostrate themselves on the stone where the body of our Lord was laid, and to us it appeared the supreme moment of their lives; they kissed it rapturously, and with an emotion seldom seen.

We soon approached Bethany and stopped to visit the Tomb of Lazarus, where Christ raised him from the dead, and the house of Mary and Martha, also the house of Simon the Leper, and a dirtier and harder looking set of humanity is seldom seen on this green earth.

We got back and Mama was never so tired in her life, and as soon as we had dinner went to bed, for the road was very rough and up and down. Next morning determined to see all of interest we started for the pools of Solomon and Bethlehem, which is directly south of Jerusalem. About one mile out is the plains where David repeatedly fought and defeated the Philistines, and about two miles out is where the Wise Men from the East, drinking from the well, saw the Star of Christ again and started with renewed courage to find Him, and it went before them until they came to where the young child was.

We soon came to the Tomb of Rachael, where the favourite wife of David was buried, and about six miles out came to Solomon's pools, three large enclosures about 200 feet square, where were held water from a spring and conveyed through earthen pipes to Jerusalem, and now the water from this spring goes to Jerusalem in 4-inch iron pipes. This is a good piece of masonry and showed that they knew all about engineering in that day. On our way back we went to Bethlehem, and in the Church of the Nativity saw the place where Christ was born, and it appears to be authenticated that this was the actual place; the exact spot which was pointed out to us may not be it exactly, but I believe this was the stable in the underground inn, and the evidence to me is conclusive as the church is now built around it and occupied by the Greeks, Catholics, and Armenians, and with great jealousy, so that their priests often come to blows, one feeling imposed upon by the other.

The manger part is about 50 ft. square and the churches of the different faiths are built on three sides of this 50 feet, and this 50 feet is guarded day and night by Turkish soldiers who are Mohammedans and have no interest except to keep the peace, and so careful are they that when a guard is relieved he goes around with a lighted candle to be sure that not even a nail is removed or disturbed.

We saw the changes of the guard. We also saw the place where Joseph was warned by the Angel at night in a vision to take the young child to Egypt. These, to us, sacred scenes were marred by the dirty streets and beggars, and by the shop-men who were determined to make us enter their shops and see their wares. We felt we wanted to be alone, and try and carry ourselves back in imagination to that time when the Child who was to redeem mankind was born, and the circumstances of the slaughter of innocents. Well, on our way back we saw the field of Boaz, where Ruth gleaned, and from the look of it thought if she got all that the field produced it would not be much.

Well, this brings me down to the noon of the 18th and Mama is so tired she has got to rest, so will close with much love to all of you and you are all well and happy.

Jerusalem, March 20, 1904

Loved Ones Five Thousand Miles Away:
This is a beautiful Sunday morning but it is somewhat hard to keep track of the Sundays, for the Mohammedans keep Friday, the Jews Saturday,

and the Christians, which comprises the Roman Catholics, the Greek Armenians and the Protestants, keep Sunday as we do, and as this place has about 40,000 Jews of the 60,000 people it makes it appear as though there was no Sunday at all.

Well we have changed our programme and will go from here straight to Constantinople and leave here tomorrow morning by the steamer *Maria Theresa*, and arrive there on Friday, 25th. We do this as we are afraid the trip will be too much for Mama, as it would be almost constant donkey and carriage for almost two weeks, and would make it almost a toil of pleasure, and too hard work for her.

We have been well so far and do not want to take any risks of over-exertion. The only thing we are lost about is our mail as this will shorten our trip some week or two and we will have to have our mail forwarded. We still are blessed with beautiful weather, not having seen any rain since our first visit to Cairo. It is cool nights and mornings in the shade, but warm in the middle of the day.

Yesterday we visited the Church of Doloroza. This is a Catholic Church built over the spot where the judgement seat of Pilate was, and was built about fifty years ago, and there can be seen the old arch under which Pilate sat in judgement of our Saviour. We also saw the old floor which is about seven feet below the present floor of the church, and also the spot where the Roman soldiers threw dice for his vestature. This is well authenticated both by history and tradition, and there can be little doubt of its correctness. We also saw the home of Pilate about 20 feet away – now occupied by Turkish soldiers just as it was by Roman soldiers in former days. This is the house where the wife of Pilate warned him to let Christ alone.

We passed the different stations now occupied by churches or benevolent institutions, showing the journey from the condemnation hall to the place of crucifixion. We went from there to the wailing wall of the Jews; they are not permitted to have a place of worship inside the walls of the city, so they meet at a place on the outside of the wall near where the temple stood and weep and wail and bump their heads against the wall, and hope and pray that God will restore to them their former city and in its greatness, and it is quite an impressive sight for you cannot doubt their sincerity, and hope that in some way God will answer their prayers and again restore Jerusalem in its former greatness and glory to them.

Sometimes your feelings are carried somewhat above the things of time and scene in reviewing these ancient and important places, and you feel you are nearer the divine presence and all at once you will feel outraged by the actions of those around and in charge of them. For instance at the Church of Doloroza I sat and was carried back to the trial of Christ and in imagination saw Pilate in his judgment seat and the High Priest clambering against Him, and crying 'Crucify Him,' and the soldiers throwing dice for his vestments, and when our feelings were most acute we were brought back by the nuns in charge bringing out a lot of beads and trash of one kind and another and trying to drive as good a bargain as they could. I felt like taking a whip and driving them all out myself. And the beggars are something awful. I thought it would not cost a great deal to give away a good quantity of coppers of which it takes three to make a cent, so got quite a lot for that purpose and started to do it, and after I had given one or two, I was fairly encircled with them coming from all directions and it was impossible to get rid of them following you for blocks, and wailing and crying until my heart was hardened and I now will not give any except I am sure no others are around. They will follow a carriage for half a mile crying 'backshief,' until you are sick and tired of the sight of them.

This afternoon we go to the Mount of Olives and the Garden of Gethsemane and this will end our sightseeing here, and really we will be glad to shake the dust of this Holy City off our feet, for while we have seen more than we ever expected to see in our lives, yet the filth, poverty and degeneration, and yet the honesty of the faith of the people, particularly the pilgrims, who have trudged thousands of miles and perhaps spent the accumulation of almost a life time, and see what they must have suffered to accomplish this, the one hope of time and eternity to see with what fervour and emotion they throw themselves and kiss the stone where the body of Christ was laid, is something that can only be seen here, and must be seen to be appreciated and understood, and yet this country is poverty in the extreme, for I never saw a farm in New Hampshire that could compare with it for stones, which are being deserted by young men and women as not fruitful enough to stay and cultivate.

Well, I have about emptied my budget and brought our trip down to this morning. I truly hope this will find you all in good health and recovered from the effects of that long, cold, hard winter, that the ice is

Master Mariner James Lough. Born in Eyemouth in 1857, he and his family moved to America before returning to Scotland where he founded a successful coastal trading business.

Above. Eyemouth Harbour
on the eve of the 1881
Fishing Disaster

Left. Memorial to the 189
east-coast fishermen lost
in the 1881 Disaster

Top. A steam drifter similar to the *Maggie Lough* approaching Eyemouth

Above. Three old men at the pierhead in Eyemouth. The man on the right is John Purves, who came home from America after just three months.

Top. The Lough family home at 17 George Street, Eyemouth

Above. The original Craig home in Coldingham. This picture was taken
in 1926 by John Franklyn Craig. The man at the door is James Lough.
(Courtesy of Bowling Green State University, Ohio (BGSU))

Opposite. George Craig, the original migrant who left
Coldingham, Berwickshire in 1827 *(BGSU)*

James Lough and family in Toledo, Ohio

Top. James and Maggie Lough's daughters in traditional fisher lassie outfits.
(Left to right:) Jean, Jamesena, Agnes

———————

Above. Six of James and Maggie's seven children.
(Left to right:) James, Agnes, Jean, Jamesena, George, with baby John in the centre

John Craig, aged 21 *(BGSU)*

Captain John Craig in later life *(BGSU)*

Top. The Maumee River in Toledo, Ohio. The Craig shipyard is
across the frozen ice. *(Ken Dickson)*

Above. The Craig shipyard, Toledo, c. 1900 *(BGSU)*

Top. Opening of the entrance to Long Beach, California, 1909.
The beginnings of the massive Craig yard at the port. (*Elmar Baxter*)

Above. John Franklyn Craig and employees at the Craig Yard, Long Beach (*Elmar Baxter*)

Top. Launch of SS *Edgar St Vance* from the Craig shipyard, Long Beach, 1913 (*Elmar Baxter*)

Above. Workers at the Craig shipyard, Long Beach in the early twentieth century (*Elmar Baxter*)

Top. The Toledo home of the children of Willie Purves

Above. The author and Patricia Smethurst at the cleared site
of the home of James Lough in Toledo

Top. Craig Yard, Long Beach, 1938 (navy ships in the bay)

Above. Port of Long Beach Harbor Commission in 1973. James Craig is on the extreme left.

Top. James Gourlay Craig junior and the author.
In the background is the Cunard liner the *Queen Mary*, which James Craig was
instrumental in bringing to Long Beach in 1967.

Above. Toledo shipyard as it is in 2004. James Lough helped build this dry dock.

Margaret Purves Dale Waddell and the author

all out, that its effects are gone, that 100 is launched and prospects are good for this summer's work, and Alfred and Mary moved into the new house and are happy in it, and one and all are happy and well. If I could I would bring a donkey for Mama to introduce a new fashion in Madison Street, for she is quite a rider.

Well, with our hearts teeming over with love for you all, we remain,

March 23, 1904

Dear Ones, One and All:
I think I closed my last letter with an account of the wailing Jews. On Sunday we went to the Mount of Olives. We went around the west wall, passed the Damascus Gate, through the Tropian Valley between Mount Moriah and Mount Zion.It adjoins the Valley of Jebrosiphat, and visited the Tomb of the Kings built by Queen Helena, mother of Constantine the Great, and it showed us just how stones were placed against tombs. A recess was cut into the rock about two feet wide and a round stone four feet in diameter and two feet thick was put in the recess and when the tomb was to be closed this stone was rolled on edge in front of the hole of the tomb, and sealed there.

We then went to the place where the Saviour mounted his donkey to go into procession to Jerusalem. We then went to a Roman church on the top of the Mount of Olives, this is in the form of a square, about seventy-five feet on each side and a circle on each side about fifteen feet or twenty feet in diameter, and this so came together in the roof as to firm half globes all around and ending in a dome for the roof of the centre making an elegant building, and elegantly embellished with beautiful paintings and frescoes so the effect was grand and inspiring.

We then went to the hill of evil where the plot was made to destroy our Lord. We saw from there the village of Beth Page where the donkey was taken from our Lord on the ride to Jerusalem. Here, from this elevation, we also got a good view of the Dead Sea and the River Jordan. Saw the place where all the churches agreed our Lord Ascended to Heaven. Also saw the place where the Lord taught the Apostles His prayer. This is now enclosed by a wall about one hundred feet square and an elegant garden, kept up by the donation of an English lady, and on the inside of the wall are thirty-two tablets, about eight feet by five feet –

and on them are painted the Lord's Prayer in twenty-two different languages. Here also is where Christ foretold to his Apostles the destruction of Jerusalem. We saw Mispah, where Solomon was crowned king, and then went to the Garden of Gethsemane, which is near the foot of the Mount of Olives. It is now a garden about two hundred feet square and surrounded by a beautiful iron fence, the garden is beautifully laid, and on the walk outside are fourteen carvings to represent fourteen different scenes in the life of our Saviour, from His ministry to His crucifixion. Here are two old olive trees about ten feet in diameter, believed to have been there at this historic time, as they are said to live almost forever. We were shown the place believed to be the place where Judas betrayed our Lord with a kiss. We then went to the Tomb of the Virgin Mary, cut out of a solid rock sixty-three steps below the road, and made beautiful by an altar and over five hundred silver lamps presented by some religious persons. We returned home made sad by the sight of so many lepers beggars by the way, and we gave them all the small change we had, and they clambered for more.

This ended our sight seeing in Judea and on Monday morning we took an early train for Jaffa, and there embarked in a big steamship *Kaiserin Maria Theresia* for Constantinople via the island of Rhodes and Smyrna. The island of Rhodes is famous for its statuary, both in marble and bronze. The celebrated statue of Colussus, when taken down and sold, took seven hundred camels to carry it away.

We got there early Tuesday morning, but there was such a sea on we did not land, but it was a beautiful sight, as it is built on a gentle sloping hill facing the east and we saw it in the morning (8 a.m.) with a good strong sun shining on the white houses it was a pretty sight indeed.

Well, it is now noon of that day and we are going pleasantly up the Grecian Archipelago, passing islands like the Thousand Islands of the St Lawrence, only the islands are larger and mountainous, snow being seen on some of the peaks of Asia Minor.

We left our party at Jerusalem as we were afraid Mama could not stand the hard riding we would have going to Nazareth, and with another of the party will go over all the ground of the trip except Nazareth, but by this means our trip will be cut short some twelve or fifteen days, as we took a fast steamer and will not be some ten days going to Constantinople. We will now end our party trip we think on April 5th at Naples. By this means we are afraid we will not get any of our mail sent to Jerusalem or after that until we get to Paris, where we will have it forwarded to. While we have not decided we now think our itinerary from the 5th April will be: We will leave Naples April 7th and go to Rome, leave there April 11th and go to Florence, leave there and go to Milan on April 13th, leave Milan on the 15th and go to Paris April 16th, stay there about a week and maybe longer and go to London about the 22nd or 25th and stay there a week or ten days, and then go up to Liverpool, Edinburgh and maybe run over to Eyemouth and see the Loughs, and leave Glasgow for home on the steamer *Columbia* on May 14th. Now, while these are our present thoughts we possibly might change them, and if tired of Paris sooner then expect to go to London sooner, and not go any further north and come home from there on April 29th on the St. Paul with John Hunter the engineer.

Well, love to all as if named.

Constantinople, March 28, 1904

Much Missed and Loved Ones, Big and Little, That Means Even the Babies:

I think I closed my last about our passing the Island of Rhodes. Well, we continued on through the Aegean Sea passing all the historic islands such as Patros, where John wrote the Revelations; Samos, noted in ancient Greek history, and arrived at Smyrna about 9 a.m. the morning of the 24th. It is up a bay some thirty or more miles and little towns on each side of it. Here it was a little cold, it rained with us last night, but it was evidently snow here for the mountains of Asia Minor were all snow capped, but a bright sun soon made it disappear. This is well fortified and is the largest city and most important in Asiatic Turkey, noted for its rugs.

We went ashore and took a carriage ride through the city which is more European than any we have seen since leaving Naples. This city looks much better from the steamer than when you go through it, for it is dirty, streets narrow and nothing inviting to an American except the houses built on the edge of the bay. All the windows are latticed so the women can look out and not be seen. One of the differences between these women and ours, is – they, the women here, cover their faces entirely so they can not be seen at all and do not care if their legs are exposed to the knee or higher, while our women are just the reverse.

We looked over some beautiful and costly rugs but Mama could not enthuse over them, she could not see any $200 in a little rug 10 x 12 feet because it was 75 or 100 years old, so we will not bring any rugs home with us.

We left there about 6 P.M. and about 6 o'clock the next morning entered the far-famed Dardanelles; it is a strait like the Narrows below New York. Here we took a pilot and after being inspected continued on our course. About eight miles above it is a rendezvous of some twelve or fifteen vessels of war, part of them battleships. The scenery is beautiful, it being a clear sunshiny morning.

We came on through the Sea of Marmora without incident, and about 3 p.m. came to the great Constantinople, this hot-bed of crime and deviltry of every description. It is at the entrance of the Sea of Marmora, the same as Gibraltar is to Lake Erie, and it is built on the side and top of a hill, and the stream or indentation of the Golden Horn almost divides it in two parts; on one side is the European quarter called Pera, and on the other the more Turkish and called Stamboul. There are other quarters called Galatea and Seutari. The Mosques with the Minarets make the water an imposing appearance, making it look like a city of churches and very beautiful when the sun shines on them.

As it was some 3 p.m. when we reached the city, as soon as the formalities of the customs were through, we steamed up the Bosporus to the Black Sea and it is a beautiful sail, palaces and country villas on each side, and fortifications every few miles and the river bends in reaches here and there and the forts can rake any boat fore and aft before they come broadside on. It looks as though they could sink the navies of the world before they could pass either the Bosporus or Dardanelles. I think the Black Sea is about twenty-five miles from the city. We went up it a few miles and then returned to the city and got to our Hotel about 7 p.m.

The first thing that impressed us was the dogs, here, there and everywhere, and they are protected by law as scavengers of the city. They are curs with long noses as though some time they came from wolves. Mama counted fourteen in one block, and they were lying around everywhere, and our guide told us they had certain limits and if a strange dog came where he did not belong, the dogs of that section would attack him and almost eat him up. I thought I would like to have old Jack here a little while and see him eat up a hundred or two for a meal, for at night when forty or fifty of them get barking it is something terrible to listen to.

Well, we got a good dinner and a good night's rest here at the 'Pera'. Our baggage got here in good shape next morning and we started to do the Mosques. The first visited was St. Sophia, said to be the largest in the world, it is capable of giving standing room to 28,000 persons. It formerly was an Armenian church and when Constantinople was taken by the Turks from the Byzantines, the Sultan rode right into it and destroyed the images of Mary and the Lord with his sword and it was altered into a Mosque, and all paintings covered up as there can not be any paintings in a Mosque. The columns supporting some of the galleries are of different kinds of stones and most of them were taken from the Temple of Diana at Ephesus where Paul preached. The pulpit is an exact representation of the one at the grand Mosque at Mecca. We went to the fountain given by the Emperor William on his visit here a few years ago, and here stands the mate of the obelisk which stands in Central Park, New York.

We visited the National Museum and all the curiosities excavated in Syria and Asia Minor, consisting of the sarcophagus of Alexander the Great and Constantine, and a lot of great men of ancient times, some of them wonderful in the artistic carvings of times and scenes in their lives; a great many statues of Nero, his wife, and most of the gods of heathen mythology are seen here. Went to the Mosque of Adamedia, only a little smaller than the last but more gorgeous in embellishments. The windows are very fine and the rugs covering the floor are the finest that can be produced. Also visited Mosque of Salemania, also beautiful, but Mosques are plentiful here of all sizes and kinds, and in all states of repair, some almost ruins.

We visited the tombs of the Sultans, and the thoughts of that is that they are sincerely mourned for a little while and then the tombs allowed to soon become ruins. We went to the Museum of Janissaries; they were a class who made and unmade Sultans at their pleasure. When tired of a Sultan they raised a revolt and killed him and before he could think of anything he was gone and another in his place.

On Sunday we went over into Asia to Sutcuria, there was a great hospital built and operated by Florence Nightingale during the Crimean War, and here is the largest burying ground in Asia, over three miles long and one mile wide and the tomb stones falling all around. Here also will be the terminus of the great railway to the East Indies via Persia.

This Monday morning we went to the Treasury, or place where all the jewels of the Sultan are kept, and it is quite a job to get there. We would not have been able to but another party got permission and we slipped in as part of that party, and it is the most wonderful collection of jewels in the world. It is estimated, if they were sold it would bring enough money to pay the whole debt of the Turkish Empire. This building has the seal of the Sultan and is guarded by over one hundred men. Before it can be opened an aide-de-camp of the Sultan must bring an order signed by the Sultan. He then breaks the seals and opens the doors, and he must stay there and seal it up again and return the seal to the Sultan, and no doubt the value has not been overestimated for of gold, silver, and precious stones I never saw such a quantity and I can not begin to describe them, accumulations of all the Sultans for hundreds of years. We spent the afternoon at the bazaars and tomorrow will sail to Athens.

April 5, 1904

Dear Ones:
We left Constantinople on the 29th as per my last letter on the good steamer *Prince Abbas* in fine weather and it was a beautiful sight, the setting sun shining on the Mosques. We arrived in Smyrna about 3 p.m., went ashore and took a ride and walked through the bazaars, and left again at 6 p.m. for Athens and arrived there at 11 a.m. next morning. The port of entry is Piris and is about six miles from Athens, which we got to by carriage; and when you read and think of the ancient history of Athens and Greece you say, 'How the mighty have fallen'. It is hard to realize that she was the mistress of the world and the center of all culture and learning.

In the afternoon we went to the Temple of Minerva and Jupiter, The Acropolis, and Mars Hill, where Paul preached from. The prison where Socrates was confined and poisoned. Climbed to the Parthenon, and Temple of Wingless Victory, and tried to realize their splendours when in their full glory. Also went to the Stadium where 40,000 people were assembled to see the ending of the great Olympium races. It has just been rebuilt at a cost of $2,000,000 out of Pentelins marble, a present from some man whom I thought had more money than he knew what to do with, for it may be visited by perhaps some fifty people per day, but had he built it in London, Paris or even New York at least five hundred would enjoy it. It would make an excellent dry dock 750 feet long, 200 feet wide at the bottom, and 40 at the top and all out of marble, and each stone perfectly fitted you could not put your knife point in it. It seats forty thousand people and great festivities will be held here next year.

We spent the morning looking at shops and the museums, and all museums are much the same – statuary, and some of it by the great masters. The most interesting things we saw there were monuments removed from the oldest known cemetery, elegant carvings in slabs, and represented the departed shaking hands and bidding adieu to friends; some of them were bestowing their jewels to sons and daughters, and most of them describing their bidding good-bye to things on earth.

Our hotel was close to King George's palace and we saw him and also the Crown Prince; they are very democratic. When they leave the palace trumpets sound and the guard present arms; they do not have any soldiers attending them. It was so that the Crown Prince was looking our way and he bowed to us and we returned the salute. The dress of his guard is very peculiar. They are Albanians and have a kind of a skirt or coat coming half way down the thigh and a tight fitting pair of drawers or stockings going down to their shoes and on the toe of the shoe a tuft of hair looking almost like a rosette, and at a distance you might easily think them women with short skirts.

We made a visit to the ruins of the Temple of Eluesis and Apollo and Dalphne on the Bay of Salamis. Here was fought the great battles of the Greeks under Themistocles and the Persians under Xerxes in the fifth century before Christ, ending in the defeat of the Persians, and the ascendancy of the Greeks. Here was the mysteries of Eluesis carved under this temple. Here Hyapatia was initiated in those mysteries in the hope of scaring her to death, but she was a woman of fortitude and afterward gave it all away when she was safe from harm, she was the favorite of Pericles.

We saw Corinth on the road where Paul wrote his epistle to the Corinthians. Saw the Temple of Pluto, the King of Hades. We saw also the Negara, where once a year the young girls dance before the young men desiring wives, and a young man desiring a young woman throws his hat in front of her and if she picks it up it is an engagement.

Well, we left Athens Sunday morning on the steamer *Niger* for Naples where we expect to arrive at 5 o'clock tonight, and will follow out the program I gave you in our last. We now expect to sail from Glasgow May 14th on steamer *Columbia*. We had quite a dead sea after leaving Sunday and Mama was a little sick but is now all right.

Have just passed Stromboli, the volcano, but it is not very boisterous this morning, just a little smoke coming from it.

We have not had any letters since leaving Cairo the 13th March and are hungry for some; hope they will be forwarded to us in Paris. Hope you are all well, see by a London paper a great tornado in Detroit, hope it did not reach you. Well love to all, we remain,

Rome, April 9, 1904

Dear Ones at Home:

My last told you we arrived in Naples on the night of the fifth. After a good night's rest which braced Mama up, we started around the city, and as we were here before we knew how and where to go to see what was wanted to, and concluded by noon we had enough so at 3 p.m. started for the Eternal City of Rome, where we arrived about 8:20. As this was our first travelling alone we did not know how we would get along, but knowing what hotel we were going to we did not have any trouble, and at the 'Mickel' we again found a good bed and enjoyed it.

The scenery from Naples to Rome is good, from smoking Vesuvius, which was putting out a lot of smoke and as we passed it, it was with awe for we felt life and death was in its power and the cause was yet to be found out. The fields were a beautiful green and trees in blossom, and every part of it so perfectly clean, no weeds or fences to mar the view, and a good many little villages on the mountain sides, which in the sun made a beautiful picture; and the clothes of the natives are so picturesque, no matter how ragged they may be, yet the colors are so bright and varied as to show their tastes, and no naked people, so different from what we have been looking at for this last two months.

We started out to Rome, and of course the first thing was St. Peters, and it was wonderful and magnificent. The proportions are so grand; why our capitol at Washington would just make a good office for it. It is in the shape of a cross, with one of the legs twice as long as the other so that the proportions are just like any cross that people wear around their necks, and the long way is over 600 feet, so that from one end looking to the other a man looks like a small boy, and it is a hard job to give even a faint idea of the beauty of it. It has about twenty altars in it, and the carvings are masterpieces of art, and all the great pictures of Michelangelo and the great masters are copied in mosaic, and so perfect is this work as to make it hard to believe it is done in mosaic work. The domes, for there are a lot of them, are also in mosaic for no paintings are allowed.

The tombs, or sarcophagus, of the different Popes are wonderful works of art, and the whole thing has cost up to this time over seventy million of dollars, and it is not and never will be finished, for when one part is complete, the other parts want to be gone over again.

The present Pope has not been in it since his election, and will visit it on Monday. We will not see him for the crowd will be something awful. They are now putting up fences all over it to control the crowd and give room for the procession from the Pope's palace to his throne. Statues and mosaics of all the Apostles are all over, but one we looked at in particular, for it was a bronze of St. Peter, and nearly all the toes of one foot were worn off by the faithful kissing it. I think one thousand people were there while we were but it was almost empty.

The city is full of visitors, tourists, and a great many pilgrims. I would say at least 20,000 were here like ourselves to see and be seen, for at the catacombs I think there were over one hundred carriages full of people, and Rome without the tourists would be nowhere for they are making out of the tourists I think at least $100,000 a day.

After we were tired of walking around in this big place we went to the Hall of Statuary, and the amount of money and labor to produce this finished product can hardly be computed, for as you look at and study the details of some of these great works of art you can hardly conceive of the patience necessary to accomplish it. I know I never could think of finishing one of them in my life time. And they are by the hundreds, I might say by the thousands. We drove up on one of the great hills to have good look of the city, and there was a park there full of beautiful carriages and men and women and a band, which any bandmaster might be proud of. Mama enjoyed it immensely and was not as tired as I thought she would be.

Yesterday we went to the Sistine Chapel, and you had a queer feeling as you enter it. This is the place where the Cardinals are locked in at the death of a Pope until another is elected, and that being so recent gave it new interest to us. It is a bare room so far as furniture is concerned, about 60 x 40 feet, and a bench seat all around it, and looks bare, but the walls are magnificent. On one end is the famous picture of the Judgement by Michelangelo, and it is a study for a day or a week before you would fully comprehend all the figures. Above in the first place is the great Judge sitting in judgement and the world going in front of Him, some to heaven, some to purgatory, and some to Hades, and angels of light and darkness pushing and leading to their respective places. One peculiar thing about it is when Michelangelo was painting it, one of the Cardinals criticized it a good deal, so Michelangelo to get even with him painted him in Hades, and the likeness was so perfect that everyone knew him as soon as it was uncovered, and it still remains so. On the sides and ceiling also are great pictures, but for a great conclave as the Cardinals make to elect a Pope, the room looks naked and no comforts, for you will remember they were locked up in this room, if I remember, for a week or more. The picture gallery is probably the greatest in the world for historic pictures and by the greatest masters, and money could not buy them. I can not begin to enumerate them in fact we became so filled with statuary and paintings we could not enjoy them as we should. One might spend a month every day in St. Peters and the two galleries and then not be acquainted with all the masterpieces.

We went in the afternoon to the Appian Way, a road built by Caesar, and also his aqueduct to bring water twenty miles to the city. Also the catacombs. These are tombs underground in streets, and the streets are altogether fourteen miles long. We went down the first course thirty-eight feet under ground, and two stories below that. Some of the martyr's tombs were elegant but Mama was glad to get out.

London, April 22, 1904

Dear Ones:

I last wrote you from Rome. Well, we did it up fully. On Saturday the ninth we went to the picture of Aurora and the Parthenon, and drove around on Sunday. Went to the M.E. Church and had a good sermon, and in the afternoon went to St. Paul's Church outside of the city, and next to St. Peter's is the greatest and most magnificent or more expensive, for it is all either marble or gold and mosaic and is wonderful to look upon. Portraits of all three hundred and over Popes in mosaic and gold, and pictures of all the Apostles and great scenes of the New Testament. I would not begin to guess the cost but it must have been at least $25,000,000. Now, there are three hundred and sixty churches in Rome and they are all magnificent but some are a great deal more grand than others. We also called at the Church of St. Peter in Chains and Capitol Hill and again at the Forum.

Well, we left Rome on Monday for Florence and were comfortably situated at the Hotel Savoy, that night we took carriages and did the town in short order. Went to the Casino, the great driving park, and the big churches and galleries of paintings and statuary, but after being in Rome we were spoiled for they all looked tame. We left Florence on a sleeper just for the experience and it was not grand except in price, for it cost about $4.00 each for a berth and poor accommodations at that, but we lived through it and arrived at Milan next morning. We only looked it over and left for Lucerne where we arrived at 2:00 p.m.

This is a beautiful place and the ride to it in daylight was splendid. Snow covered Alps on every side, and we climbed up until we had snow all around us; the waterfalls from melted snow were grand. It took us some nineteen minutes to go through St Gothards Tunnel, and when we get through what a change for it commenced to rain on the south side and on the north when we came out was nice, clear and warm sunshine. Fluma is the town on the north side and there is quite a lake there on which steamboats run to Lucerne, and it must be a beautiful sail for forty miles. Lucerne nestles in the foot of the mountains and can not hardly be described, must be seen to be appreciated. We took a ride through it and then went up an inclined railway and sat looking and admiring it for two hours. Left there at 7:30 and stopped at Basle for the night. It is the second largest city in Switzerland, some 160,000 people and is noted for its hospitality. Here they entertained some 15,000 women and children during the French and German War (of 1871), for when Strasbourg was infested they had to leave. We left this good and pretty city at 9:00 a.m. on the 14th and got to gay Paris at 7:00 p.m.

In going from Basle to Paris we go through Germany about sixty miles but we did not stop, thinking the Linn girls had done Germany well enough for the whole family. We got rooms at the Hotel Du Louvre and

I made up my mind we had to go slow for Mama was pretty nearly tired out. Here we got some of our mail we should have got in Constantinople, but not half as much as we expected. Aunt Sarah is the only one whose letters reach us regularly, we have had more from her than anyone else. Well the next day we went to the Odéon and as our Hotel is right opposite the Louvre Palace and galleries and gardens, we are right in it. We took a ride to Versailles alongside the River Seine and were astonished at the traffic on it. It is covered with beautiful bridges and public buildings are immense and being an old city, monuments abound in great profusion.

We went to the Bon Marche, and the Grand Magasin de Louvre which are noted stores of Paris, and all the noted churches as Notre Dame, St. Peters, Madeline, and the Opera House and the Column Vendôme and the Arch of Triumph. I went up in the Eiffel Tower, and it is a good way up a magnificent structure and of great stability for I could not feel the least quiver while up there, and I stayed some twenty minutes.

We are not satisfied with our letters so we hurried over to London leaving on the 19th via the New Haven and Dieppe route. This is the longest water route but it is here that they have the turbine steamers and I hoped it might be her day but it was not. We came over in the *Sussex*, a boat as big as the *Porto Rico* and with 550 H.P. She could go and she did. It was not rough but the vibration with the little sea made most of the women sick.

We have been going too fast for the last month, Mama is somewhat tired out, but if able I want her to see Edinburgh and Glasgow and then she will have a general idea of the continental cities. We arrived here last Wednesday night and have gone over considerable of it; have been to Cheapside, White Chapel, Westminster Abbey and St. Paul Cathedral, the Strand, Ludgate, Billingsgate, Waterloo, Westminster and London Bridge, and so on, but a good many more to see.

This is a wonderful large city and peculiar in a good many ways. An underground railway to take you most anywhere and street cars which do not run in the city proper, which is very small, but the old fashioned stages with seats on top, and you would be astonished to see Mama climb up there for it gives you a good view of where you are going. More ride there than inside and the charge is a penny a mile and then pay again, or tell them when you get on where you are going to and pay accordingly.

From the look of the stores you would think they were almost all tailors or jewellers, for they are in abundance.

Well, I might go on and spin this out a long way but I will quit for fear of making you tired. We are beginning to think a sight of you all will be worth more to us than all we can see, for while it has been a good trip and enjoyable yet you soon realize there is no place like home, so hoping by another four weeks we will see you all and enjoy a good kiss from all, great and small, we remain.

Reefing My Sail

On my return we continued to build boats in the Toledo yard and you, no doubt, remember a great deal about that time. One of our little ships launched in 1903 has made quite a name for herself. She was built for the Michigan Transportation Company of Michigan City and was christened the *City of Indianapolis*. A few years later she was sold to go to the Pacific Coast. She had to go around the Horn as that was in the days before the Panama Canal and she made the fastest trip ever made by a vessel her size between New York and Seattle. She is still making the run between the latter city and Tacoma, Washington.

We sold out in 1907 when your father, John F Craig, moved West and established the Craig Shipbuilding Company at Long Beach, California, so his boys would have the shipbuilding business to grow up in as he had. I retired from active shipbuilding at that time but held all my other business connections and actively managed the Adams Transportation Company and the Monroe Transportation Company with their lake boats until 1916 when we sold out. I was then eighty-eight years of age. Since then I have remained, however, on various directorates – Toledo Metal Wheel Company, now affiliated with the Gendron Company, the C.K. Merrill Company, the Society of Savings, and the First National Bank. I am the only one of the original directors of that bank living today. I have been on the board for thirty-four years, as I was put on the directorate about five years after we moved to Toledo. I have always maintained an office and gone to it every day that I have been in this city. We have made trips to California and Florida regularly and in 1916 I made a trip to Honolulu as you no doubt remember, for you were here staying with you grandmother while I was away. Your father went with me to San Francisco and introduced me to Mr. Derricks, then general manager of the Matson Navigation Company. He had been chief naval architect in the McDougal Shipyard at Duluth so knew our boats and could talk my language. He very courteously introduced me to the captain and chief engineer of the good ship *Wilhelmina* so that my voyage was a pleasant one. Your grandmother has my letters of that trip and thinks that they are very interesting. Maybe she will let you have them.

Ship Subsidy

Yes, I am still preaching ship subsidy and the rehabilitation of our merchant marine. It is my favourite subject for a speech or discussion and unless someone gives me a text when called to my feet I will talk subvention – and I should know something about it for my experience goes back to 1856, and I reason this way: Our merchant marine was destroyed by the Civil War, and by the change from wood to metal ships, when we were not an iron-producing nation. As I told you I remember when steel rails were $140.00 per ton, but since that time we have appreciably reduced the cost and I know of times when they were bought for $18.00 per ton. What caused this great reduction in cost and price? The competition of our own manufacturers, the inventive skill of our own mechanics and also the protection given that industry by our Government.

Are we a maritime people? Everybody will say yes. The proof of it is in our history before the little unpleasantness of 1861 to 1865. Our clipper ships out-sailed and out-lived the ships of any nation on earth. The records of the *Sea Witch, Flying Cloud, Challenger, Invincible, Sovereign of the Seas, Dreadnought* and fifty more I could name, and the fact that England had tried for fifty years to recapture the cup *America* won from them, show it.

Does our climate and soil and the habits of our people make us love or hate navigation? Where in the world will you find the yachting and fishing fleets that we have, the coasting vessels so adapted for this work? – and yet, to think that this great, glorious country, with thousands of miles of sea coast, a population of one hundred and ten million people, needing to buy and sell in the markets of the world, furnishes only eight to ten per cent of our own sea transportation and expends from four to six hundred million dollars annually with other nations that receive all the profit out of it in building, supplying and manning this needed marine.

I believe the United States is determined to have a merchant marine;

cost what it will. We must look upon our marine as an infant industry, and our Government must encourage and protect it until it is demonstrated that our country and the habits of our people are not in harmony with commerce and transportation. We must do as a man does with his infant son – first carry him, then lead him, then teach him, and by that means make a man of him. So it should be with our merchant marine – we must protect it against the cheap, under-paid labor of Europe and Asia, and if necessary by subsidy and subvention. If by discriminating duties, so be it, and if needed to find out if we can make a success of it we should as a last resort forbid the ships of any nation from importing or exporting our goods except to and from the nation to which the ship belongs. We could in ten or twenty years at the farthest demonstrate that we have or have not the brains, the muscle, the business acumen to in a measure control our transportation and commerce. Give us this opportunity, and I believe we will again build ships for the world.

I have a record of building one hundred and seven vessels before I reached the sere and yellow leaf, and then did not stay there, for I was one of the dollar a year helpers in the late [Great]war. If experience amounts to anything, I have had it.

I am now in my ninetieth year, but would like to see, before I go to the great beyond, the merchant marine of our country, which I love, as I did see it from 1850 to 1865.

I cannot help thinking of the illustration of protection by Abraham Lincoln. He was asked his opinion of protection and tariff and he said, 'I feel this way about it. If I go to England and buy a pair of pants and pay $10.00 for them, it is a fair, square trade. They have the $10.00 and I have the pants. But if I have them made at home we have the pants and the $10.00 too!' That is a homely argument which cannot be gainsaid.

He Leadeth Me

EDITOR'S NOTE, BY RUTH CRAIG MERRELL:

I am firmly convinced that the power, the poise and the serenity of my Grandfather have come to be a part of him because of his devout faith in a great and guiding Deity. His spirit of humility and everlasting thankfulness is so beautifully expressed in the prayers each Sunday morning at family worship that I here print without his knowledge these words of praise and supplication as I heard them from his lips on a beautiful Sabbath in the Spring of 1928 when I was privileged to be one of his household.

A PRAYER:

'Almighty Father and Giver of every good and perfect gift, again on this first day of the week we bow now at Thy footstool and in Thy goodness and mercy thank Thee that we are all present once more to call upon Thee for aid throughout another week. Truly we have been the creatures of Thy compassion. Truly goodness and mercy has followed us all of our days. We enjoy associations of friends and relatives that are joined to us by ties of blood and we thank Thee for Thy care over them. Give us thankful hearts and allow us to rejoice. Bless our friends and relatives wherever they may be on land or sea, on plain or mountain. Be Thou then good and guide and direct them in Thy ways. Forgive anything which Thou has seen amiss in us in word or deed, in action or in thought, and lead us in straighter paths throughout another week. Bless the poor and unfortunate, the sick and afflicted and suffering humanity wherever it may be found. Bless our Land and Nation. Give us good rulers of peace and of justice who will honor Thee and Thy teachings to mankind. Amen.'

Capt. And Mrs Craig Wedded 67 Years

Party Guests Presented With Volume Of His Life

"Episodes of My Life" by John Craig, was presented at the 67th wedding anniversary dinner given in honour of Capt. And Mrs John Craig, 2105 Madison Avenue, Saturday night.

The book, autographed by Capt. Craig was written for him by his granddaughter, Mrs Thomas Merrell, of Long Beach, Calif., and was compiled from stories which were told to children and grandchildren by Capt. Craig.

Capt. And Mrs Craig were married in New York, Nov. 3rd 1861. They moved to Michigan in 1866, where Capt. Craig established the first ship yards on the Great Lakes. Here he built the wooden vessels which cruised the inland seas.

In 1888 he built the Toledo ship yards, calling them the Craig ship yards, and started the building of steel ships. The family has lived at the present address on Madison Avenue for 35 years.

Capt. and Mrs Craig have two sons and one daughter living. There are ten grandchildren and six great grandchildren. All the great grandchildren live in California and came to celebrate the occasion of the 67th anniversary. Capt. Craig will be 90 on Christmas Eve.

Toledo Blade, November 1928

THE NOBLEST
WORK OF GOD

Memoirs of James Lough, Master Mariner,
Eyemouth, formerly of Toledo, Ohio

As written by him in 1929

Introduction to *The Noblest Work Of God*

Ruth Craig Merrell compiled the biography of her grandfather John Craig to present to him and to her grandmother Annie Losee on the occasion of their sixty-seventh wedding anniversary in November 1928. Only one hundred copies of the book were printed for private distribution amongst close friends and members of the family. One was sent to James Lough in Scotland. He was of course related to John Craig through his now deceased wife Maggie Purves, Craig's second cousin. James Lough visited America in 1922 and again in the spring of 1928. It was on this latter trip that he met Ruth Merrell and willingly helped her with the research for her book. The Craigs' business interests had by then moved to the west coast where John Craig's sons, John Franklyn and George Craig, had established a shipyard at Long Beach in 1907/8. John and Annie had, however, remained in Ohio.

On that long vacation in the autumn of his life, Lough spent time at his old haunts on the Great Lakes and also several weeks in California. He had been invited to visit the Pacific base by John Franklyn Craig who had made his own journey back to the ancestral home in Berwickshire in 1926.

Lough was obviously inspired by Ruth Merrell to commit his own remarkable life story to paper. But the document, which he took six months to complete, was kept secret from the rest of his family. It was unknown even to his beloved granddaughter Peggy Dale who spent many hours at James's side hearing of his adventures in America: of how he built up his little coastal trading business, of his experiences during the Great War and of the joy and sorrow that life and death had brought to his door. Those stories were passed on through the family. The oral tradition that Peggy Dale bequeathed also included horrific testimony from the Great East Coast Disaster of 1881 – and in particular the manner in which her great-grandfather James Purves had died. Purves was the skipper of the *Myrtle* and to save himself from being washed overboard he had strapped himself to the tiller of the boat. But the sea tossed the

Myrtle over in a single suffocating wave and James Purves, and the six other crewmen, were pulled down to their deaths. He left a widow, Jane Mack Purves, two sons, John and Willie, who were on another boat and somehow managed to survive the hurricane, and a daughter, Maggie Purves, who was married to James Lough.

As a boy I listened to the stories of my grandmother Peggy Dale Waddell in much the same way as she had been enraptured by the tales of her grandfather, her 'Goff', James Lough. This inspired me to write down the history of the Eyemouth Disaster and some of the other remarkable incidents that took place in that small Berwickshire town over the past five centuries. The result, *Children of the Sea: The Story of the Eyemouth Disaster* (Tuckwell Press, 2001) sold well and many copies were sent overseas. I was delighted to then hear from some of the descendants of the Berwickshire Diaspora who contacted me with questions or comments or, as was the case with Patricia Smethurst, priceless information. Patricia is the great-great-granddaughter of Peter Craig, one of the original migrants who had left Coldingham in the 1830s. He later made a fortune during the California Gold Rush of 1849. Pat provided a treasure-trove of detail about the Craig family and also, to my utter amazement, told me of the existence of a manuscript written by James Lough which is now lodged in the University of Bowling Green, Ohio.

The curator of the Great Lakes collection, Robert Graham, kindly sent me a copy. I had expected a slim document – perhaps only a page or two of script. In fact the memoirs ran to more than a hundred, tightly written pages which dripped emotion and sang out the song of the ordinary man.

Why James Lough decided against telling anyone of what he was writing will never be known. The document itself is a raw and at times disjointed account of his life and of some of the events which he experienced. It was untitled, but I have chosen to call it *The Noblest Work of God* which is a telling phrase used by Lough during his time in Toledo. I have also added chapter headings which were not in the original in order to break up the narrative and, as James himself asked of Ruth Merrell, I have slightly amended some of the text. The vast bulk of what follows however is exactly as James Lough wrote it almost eighty years ago. It was only by chance and good fortune that it survived. It is a fitting tribute to this man who was indeed the 'Noblest Work of God' that his memoirs have finally been published.

The opening two pages are letters sent by James Lough to Ruth Craig Merrell, the first to acknowledge receipt of the biography of her grandfather and the second, written six months later, as a covering note to Lough's own life story. In that first letter, sent on December 14 1928, James recalls that John Craig and Annie Losee had stayed with him in Eyemouth when they visited in 1914. It is possible that they did so, but it is more probable that James meant 1904. That was the year when John and Annie spent months touring Europe and the Holy Land before stopping off in Berwickshire en route back to the United States.

James also notes in that first letter that his next-door neighbour, George Craig of St Ella's Place, 'amongst the foremost fishermen in not only our town but our county' was a distant cousin of John Craig. Indeed he was. As was outlined in the general introduction and is noted in the genealogical diagram, George Craig's great-great-grandfather and John Craig's great-grandfather were brothers. In another twist to the tale, the grandson of George Craig of St Ella's Place, George Craig Aitchison, would come to marry James Lough's great-granddaughter, Jasmin Lough Dale Waddell, in 1959. They had four children, Martin, Elaine, Janis and me.

At the end of the memoir James tells of how during his visit to America in 1928 he was anxious to visit the Probate Court in Toledo to obtain citizenship papers for his son Jamie, who had been born in Ohio in 1893. James managed to secure the documents for the boy who was anxious 'to make his name in California'. Jamie doubtless hoped to be helped by his Craig cousins in Long Beach in much the same way as his father had been helped by that Scottish-American family in Toledo forty years earlier.

But young Jamie did not make it back to the United States. Like his brothers John and Robert, Jamie's health had been ruined from his time in the merchant fleet during the Great War. Jamie died in 1929 – just a matter of weeks after his father completed this manuscript. It was the story of James Lough senior rather than the energy of James Lough junior that found its way back to America.

Eight decades passed before James Lough's long-forgotten journal was unearthed, allowing the equally forgotten family links that had been so powerful and so sustaining to be renewed. In the spring of 2004 I visited Toledo and met with my fourth cousin Patricia Smethurst, who was brought up in California, but who now lives in Maine. Like me, this was her first visit to Toledo. Together we stood on the wharf at the former Craig shipyard on the Maumee River where once huge boats were launched to trade on the Great Lakes. After some years in the doldrums the yard is now back in business building ships which will sail across this mighty inland sea. I spoke with Jim Lynch, the assistant general manager of what is now the Toledo Ship Repair Company. He showed me the dry docks that are almost unaltered since James Lough helped build them more than a century ago.

Local historian Ken Dickson sketched the site of what must have been a mighty industrial enterprise. Next door to the shipyard was the huge Malleable Iron Works, now long gone but once the employer of hundreds of migrants from Europe. And across the road from these totems of Toledo industry is Front Street, where the families of the workers, including the family of James Lough, would have lived. It is a largely deserted and run-down part of the city these days. But in the 1890s the whole area would have teemed with people and been alive with the sounds of both work and play as the cacophony of noise from the shipyard and the ironworks competed with the raucous accompaniment of saloon bars and bordellos.

Pat Smethurst and I walked down Front Street and then paused for thought on a scratchy bit of vacant ground at the corner with York Street – the cleared site where once James Lough, Maggie Purves and their children Robert, James, Jean, Agnes and Jamesena had their home. It was a poignant moment. How different Toledo must have been when they lived there: a bustling, industrial place, at times a violent place and yet, for almost eight years, it was their everything. Had circumstances been different it would have continued as the Lough family home, as it has done for the descendants of Willie Purves who stayed on and settled. It took some detective work but I managed to trace Scott Crim, the great-great grandson of Maggie Purves' brother. Scott and his wife Tricia welcomed me into their home on the opposite side of the city of Toledo.

I then flew west from the greyness of Ohio to the sunshine and sparkle of California to meet James Gourlay Craig junior, his wife Patricia and his brother Robert. The great-grandsons of John Craig are doyens of the Long Beach community. It is a community the Craigs were in large part responsible for building. Their shipyard was the first and most important venture on this part of the Pacific seaboard.

Jim, Pat and Bob made their distant Scottish cousin very welcome indeed, even arranging for me to stay on board the *Queen Mary.* I learned a huge amount from that two-day visit – both the story of John Craig and what happened to the family after their interests were relocated to the west coast. Jim and Bob's grandfather, John Franklyn Craig, proved every bit as astute as his own father had been on the Great Lakes. He negotiated a favourable deal for the establishment of the shipyard and then, when a quarter of those local people who had subscribed to bring the enterprise to Long Beach defaulted, John Franklyn bought that portion of the land with family money. For sound financial reasons he then put this estate in the name of his wife.

The Craigs built up the yard from scrub and marsh, laying down the bedrock of prosperity for the entire Long Beach district. They did well and then quite literally struck rich where they laboured. Oil seeped out from the ground beneath them. The land, which was lodged in the name of John Franklyn's wife, now poured crude and dollars into the family fortune.

J. F. Craig and his son James Gourlay Craig said, 'We have made money from oil, we should make more in oil', and wise investments in companies like Standard Oil followed. The shipyard, though not all of the waterfront acreage, was sold in 1962. But the Craigs of Long Beach, just three or four generations from the Craigs of Coldingham – those pauperised and penniless migrants – have always recognised their good fortune. James Gourlay Craig junior, now effectively the head of the family, was born in 1925. At the time of writing he is still a fearsome golfer who plays with two artificial shoulders yet off a handicap of just twelve. He has dedicated almost his entire life to public – not political – service. Jim labours on a host of committees and has worked with the very young on Boy Scout groups to the very old in his drive to raise millions for local hospitals. He served on the Long Beach Harbor Commission and led the campaign to bring the Clyde-built liner *Queen Mary* to the port in 1967. Thirty-one years earlier, in 1936, James Lough had insisted on going to Glasgow to witness the launch of that great ship.

As with Pat Smethurst and Scott Crim, Jim, Pat and Bob Craig treated me as though they had known me all their lives. They told me their stories and listened when I, in turn, gave all that I knew about the Craigs, about James Lough and his visit to Long Beach and of how his son Jamie so nearly made it to the Sunshine State back in 1928.

As a keepsake of the visit I gave both Pat Smethurst and Jim and Bob

Craig a framed strip of the linen which had been woven by our ancestors in a little cottage in Coldingham almost two hundred and fifty years earlier. That cherished piece of cloth, kept with such reverence by Peggy Purves Lough Dale Waddell, had been handed down through the generations in Berwickshire, along with family stories that proudly spoke of the Craigs who, it was said, had made it rich in America. That tangible piece of the past is now an enduring symbol of the fresh links forged by the descendants of the Craigs and of the Loughs in Berwickshire, Ohio, Maine and California.

Peter Aitchison

Letters

17 George Street
Eyemouth
Dec 14th 1928

My Dear Ruth

I received your nice book regarding your grandfather's Life Story which is a real treat to me and mine. There are quite a number of Eyemouth folks who remember your grandfather and grandmother visiting us here, and quite a few remember your great grandfather being here on a visit. It is strange how many things there are in our experiences which refresh our memories and a number of our old Fishermen remember your great grandfather because my wife's father named his fishing boat after your great grandfather George Craig.

Then your grandfather and grandmother came here, and stayed in our home in 1904 so our neighbours remember them well, and there are lots of families here named Craig who are the offspring of your great grandfather's cousins. Our next door neighbour is one of them – a George Craig – and mind they are amongst the foremost fishermen not only in our town but in our county, so all these folks will be interested to read your book.

I would have like to have shown your father their lovely homes and also their steam fishing boats, but your father had booked rooms in Edinburgh so could not spend much time here. But the Craigs are a go ahead lot of men.

My family always called your great grandfather Uncle George. He came often to my home when we lived in Toledo. He was a tall smart man, straightforward, and he always gave me the impression that he feared not any man's frown neither would he court any man's smile.

I am sorry I did not stay a few days longer while you were compiling your book. Some things have come into my memory which both of your ancestors told me which might have enhanced and added interest but it is inspiring and makes me glad that I spent so many hours in the company of such men as your two worthy sires George & John Craig.

17 George Street
Eyemouth
July 1929

My Dear Friend Mrs Merrell
I have sent to your address the story of a few incidents which happened to me during my voyage through life. I fully expect you will have some difficulty to piece it together and make it so folk can read it. There were quite a few more items I might have written but I felt ashamed to state so often that I did this or I did that, so I hope you will be able to put the writing in better form, so that the second or third person make take the place of I.

Of course if you consider it is not interesting reading, just drop it into the waste paper basket.

I sincerely hope you are all well and enjoying each others company. I hope you received the little book I sent you and I am sure if you understand the Scotch dialect then you will enjoy the book.

I am pleased to say our town is very busy at present. Of course this is our best time for herring fishing, and we have large crowds of visitors from Edinburgh. They are enjoying themselves here, watching our fisher girls packing herring into barrels. These folk find great pleasure in watching our fishing fleet going out to sea and coming in each morning with their good catches of sixty or seventy thousand herrings. We are having very fine weather at present, which we appreciate very much seeing the summers are often very short in this part of the world.

Sorry to say the great army of cotton workers are threatening to strike, which will be very serious indeed seeing there are five hundred thousand 'workers'. It seems there are no end to the troubles in our country and the wonder is how we manage to get along so well as we do.

If you have the time to spare kindly drop me a note to let me know whether you think this work which I am encumbering you with is worth the trouble it will cost you.
Kindly excuse this from your
  Sincere Friend
  James Lough

To Be My Own Master

James Lough was born to be a fisherman. It was all there was in the Berwickshire town of Eyemouth in the mid-nineteenth century. His home was a rough and unyielding place where violence and alcohol were as much a feature of life as the daily fish auctions on the pier. There was no restraining influence from religion. Churches and ministers were shunned. Eyemouth was a byword for heathenism, lawlessness and profanity. In many ways it was the mirror image of the American mid-west that James would later settle in.

Lough's decision, to shun whisky and embrace God, is therefore all the more remarkable.

He was the eldest of seven children and as such had responsibilities and expectations from the time he could walk. James would have 'minded' the other bairns when his mother, Agnes Windram, was away for long hours at a time picking shellfish to be used as bait on his father Robert Lough's lines. Later, from about the age of six or seven, James too would have tramped up to ten miles a day through freezing rock pools to harvest limpets and mussels which he then opened and attached to the thousand hooks of the haddock lines.

Before he became a teenager James would have been made a man in a 'Brothering.' This ritual involved fear and strong drink as young boys were made to stand before the assembled men of the fleet in a dank and oppressive fish-house and forced to eat salt rolls and drink whisky. Once accepted into the world of fishermen, James would have been sent to work as a cabin boy on another family's boat. Sons never sailed with fathers in the beginning. They had to be toughened up for their life ahead and given no favours when at sea.

Young James suffered terribly on his first few 'trips'. But these experiences hardened him and helped map out what he wanted to do with his life. He wanted to succeed: to be his own man. By the age of twenty James had bought his first boat and two years later he married his childhood sweetheart Maggie Purves. Lough's prospects seemed as hopeful as the boundless ambition held by the little burgh of Eyemouth. But a further two years on and those 'prospects', both for James Lough and his home community, were shattered.

James was deeply affected by the events of October 14 1881, a day which will always be referred to in Eyemouth as 'Black Friday', as 'Disaster Day'. He survived the smashing impact of the hurricane when it ripped through the Eyemouth fishing fleet. But he returned to a town that was devastated. He must have been seared by the experience of surviving – and, perhaps, of watching – as so many of his friends and relatives drowned before his very eyes. Like most who had lived through that day, James Lough rarely mentioned it in the family and he hardly touches upon it within his memoirs. Yet apart from the loss of his wife's father James Purves, who was the skipper of the Myrtle, we know that at least three of James's uncles perished – his father's brother Jimmy Lough went down with the Lily of the Valley and two of his mother's brothers also died: John Windram who was on the Radiant which was swamped on the approaches to the harbour, and James Windram who was lost on Six Brothers.

But Eyemouth was – and still is – nothing if not an extended family of just a few names and blood lines. Lough would have felt for every one of the 129 men who did not return from the ocean that day.

May 30th 1929

I James Lough, Master Mariner of 17 George Street, Eyemouth, Berwickshire Scotland was born in 1857 at Eyemouth.

My father and mother were fisher folk. I went to sea before I was twelve years old in a fishing boat. I suffered much with seasickness and the crew treated me very harshly. I had no oilskin clothes or sea boots and on that account I was drenched by sea water every day when at sea.

Blyth, Northumberland was our first port of call and if I could have managed to get onshore I certainly would have tramped home. But I cried until I fell asleep. The crew were all onshore and I felt very lonely. Our next port of call was North Shields. A boy from my own town, two years my senior who was onboard another boat with his father came to see me and while we were going ashore I slipped and fell into the river. A strong current was running and I had a hard struggle for life, yet the crew never troubled about me.

I heard them say many times I would never be any good. But their words burnt into my memory and I determined to be a good fisherman and a good man in every respect and before I was twenty years old I owned a fishing boat and half a fleet of herring nets.

But none of my friends ever knew the terrible struggle I had to pay for my first boat.

The summer fishing had just finished and I had paid for my new nets and fishing lines and I only had one pound in all the world left which I could call my own. But I heard of a boat that was for sale at the Cove about twelve miles from here. She was named the *Sovereign*. The owners had ordered a new boat which was expected to be ready eight months hence, the old boat being laid up for the winter months.

I went to inspect the *Sovereign* and also the sails and the running gear. The owners told me their price for the boat was thirty pounds. That is a small sum, but fishing boats were not so large then as they are today and I expected to save thirty pounds off my winter fishing. So I felt I could buy that boat.

But I got my finger poisoned and for nearly two months I was not able to go to sea and on that account I was ten pounds short when the time came that I should pay for the *Sovereign*. And I knew no friend who would oblige me with a loan. That was the greatest trial that had come into my life up to that date, and I suffered more than I care to tell even now.

My chum noticed the change on me and pressed me hard to know what had made me so dull and quiet, and after some persuasion I told him my trouble and he told his father who came at once to help me. He gave me the ten pounds and in three months I paid him back and I never forgot him when he was old.

I sold the *Sovereign* after that first summer fishing and bought a more up to date fishing boat and many more new herring nets.

I had then reached my first goal.

I had promised my sweetheart that I would not ask her to link her life on to mine until I was a man like other men, and now I had a boat and fishing gear I could go to sea like other brave fishermen round our coast and Maggie Purves, the best woman in this world, became my wife in 1879.

I received the sum of five pounds from my mother [Agnes Windram] to pay our honeymoon expenses and away we went towards the sunny south – but we couldn't get further than Newcastle. We were afraid we might have to walk all the way home again, so were very happy amongst the miners for three or four days. We then had just enough money left to pay our train fare home.

But no Duke or Duchess were ever more happy than we were in our one room and attic house in Chapel Street in the centre of the little town of Eyemouth. We only had enough money to buy provisions to last us one week and the first day I went to sea my young wife possessed no more than sixpence. I did not own one penny. She paid four pence for a knife to shell the mussels and one penny for some other article, I cannot remember at this moment just what it was. But as she was just starting to bait my fishing line with its ten hundred hooks, she looked out our window which was opposite a confectioner shop window and there she spied some nice cake which caused her mouth to water.

She wanted the cake so much she actually rose up from the fishing line to buy a little piece but she looked on the last penny she had and said 'To spend that on myself? Never!' But her mouth still watered as she baited my line.

We made a vow together that no strong drink would ever come into our home unless ordered for trouble, yet we were both tested on the first Saturday night. For in those days the crew of each boat numbered seven men and they gathered together in one house each Saturday night to divide their weeks earning. Very often they had a large cod or ling boiled and two pounds butter melted and poured over the whole fish which was on a large platter, and alongside some new made bread. In those days all those men ate off one plate and not one man ever complained of a bad stomach. But of course everyone knows that fish likes always to be swimming, and there could never be a fish supper unless there was plenty of beer.

No one need wonder why so many tradesmen kept so friendly with the fishermen.

Well it is easy to understand how Maggie, my young wife, felt when we heard all these men coming up our stairs on that first Saturday night of our married life. I had tried my best to advise them to go to another house, but the testing time had come. The oldest man amongst the crew had been Presenter in the church for thirty years and he said 'Now then. Maggie will get a few pounds changed into silver and bring half a gallon beer and half a mutchkin of whisky.'

Poor Maggie, I can see her look imploring me to speak for her as she was remembering our vows, so I tried to muster courage. 'Now men, Maggie and I have made a vow that we will not break tonight, she will not bring strong drink here.'

But one of the crew stood up saying 'Give me a jug and a bottle and I will go for the whisky and beer'. Again I had to tell them strong drink must not come into this house. And each Saturday night the money was divided but no strong drink ever defiled our home.

And at the end of the season my wife gave me a glad surprise. She had saved twenty pounds, as week after week we pulled together. We had made up our minds to better our circumstances and we were prepared to deny ourselves in order to accomplish our aim.

Six years after we were married, that is by 1885, I owned the largest fishing boat on our coast. Of course like all other fishermen I had gains and I had losses; good seasons and poor seasons. But no matter what went wrong onboard my boat, my home was always the brightest place on earth, until our first girl Janie turned ill and died while I was at sea.

We thought then that the sun would never shine any more in our home.

On to America

In this chapter James relates how John Craig, who was a second cousin of his wife Margaret Purves, visited Eyemouth in the summer of 1888. Mr Craig was touring shipyards in Britain, gathering information and ideas for the construction of steel-hulled vessels pending the establishment of his new yard in Toledo, Ohio. The visit was also nostalgic. Craig's aunt Sarah Craig-Robertson was still alive, and living with the extended Purves-Lough family. Sarah and her sister Jean had stayed in Berwickshire when the rest of their family had made the move to the United States in the early 1830s. At the time both women were newly married. Sadly Sarah's husband, a Coldingham blacksmith called James Robertson, died leaving her a childless widow. Perhaps surprisingly Sarah did not then follow her parents and other siblings to America but chose instead to move south to be with the rest of her family in Eyemouth.

On the quayside of Eyemouth John Craig was a celebrity. He offered the prospect of work to anyone who had a mind to follow him to the United States. James did not meet John Craig at this time. He was away catching herring off Yorkshire. On his return, though, disillusioned with the poor fishing and the lack of prospects at home, Lough decided to strike out for a new life in America. He left with his two brothers-in-law, John and Willie Purves, in the late autumn of 1888. They sent no word of their intentions to John Craig, thousands of miles away in Ohio.

All three found it hard to knuckle down to the discipline of work. It was a far cry from the independence of life at sea. Within weeks the eldest of the trio, John Purves, had had enough and returned to Eyemouth – much to the disappointment of his wife who, along with the wives and families of James Lough and Willie Purves, was all prepared to follow her man and emigrate.

James did not expect to spend so much time working for John Craig. It was always his intention to get a start on the steamers that run across the Great Lakes. But for the sake of making money which he then sent back to Scotland, he was glad enough to find employment at the Toledo shipyard – though more than a little perturbed when he discovered his duties meant he would have to carry a firearm . . . and be expected to use it if necessary . . .

But James hankered to be on a boat again and after working for John Craig for just under four years he arranged to join a trading ship en route for Duluth, far away at the head of Lake Superior. Through bad luck he missed the ship as it departed – taking with it all of his clothes. Perhaps embarrassed to ask for his old job back, Lough was hired as a common labourer at the Malleable Iron Works, which was next to the Craig shipyard and opposite his home on the corner of Front and York Street in Toledo.

Fishing became poor for a few years and I was away at Scarborough in Yorkshire when Mr John Craig, Ship Builder Toledo Ohio U.S.A. came to this country on business. He was my wife's father's cousin and he came to Eyemouth to see his Aunt Sarah. My two brothers in law, John and Willie Purves asked Mr Craig if he would give them work, he promised he would if he had any work when they came to USA and he promised Maggie to do the same for me if I came too.

And in middle of October forty years ago my brothers-in-law and I sailed from Glasgow onboard the Anchor line steamer *Grecian* bound for Montreal. While taking cargo onboard at the tail of the bank one sailor turned sick and was put onshore at Greenock. The captain did not want to go ashore, it being evening, and he asked me to take the man's place, to which I agreed.

We were nine days on the voyage. Then we went by train to Windsor, then across river to Detroit where I called at number ninety-nine, Woodward Avenue, home of the Gourlay brothers who were natives of Edinburgh. These men treated us kindly.

We had tea at Mr James Gourlay's home when we met Mr Craig. I had never met him until that date. A short while after tea we went by steamer to Trenton, sixteen miles from Detroit down the river. We arrived there after four p.m. and spent the evening with Mr & Mrs Craig at their home.

During the conversation Mr Craig said 'Well I suppose you boys have come here to get a few dollars?' We said 'Yes that is why we are here.' 'Well' he said, 'you will not find them on the ground but they are on the trees.'

I said 'I understand you Mr Craig, you mean we will have to reach for them' And we proved his words true.

Many years later Mrs Craig told me the conversation which passed between her and Mr Craig that same evening after we left their home. Mr Craig said 'Now Mrs, you must not expect all three men to stay here. Some of them will go home again.'

Mrs Craig replied 'I don't care very much who goes home if James will stay here.'

I asked Mrs Craig why she said that, and she told me she could not account for it, but she just wanted me to stay.

We started work on that first Monday. We were strong and fresh after our voyage across the Atlantic. It was election time and lots of men were idle on that account. We were anxious to do a big days work and that took away our judgement. We had been at sea since we were boys and had very little idea of any kind of work onshore and I am certain if the whistle for dinner had been five minutes later in sounding all three of us would have lost our work.

We had not done the job properly and were very sorry. However two Frenchmen who had always worked in shipping were sent to work along with us that afternoon and we did much better.

But I felt it very hard to be ordered round sometimes by labourers after I had been master of my own boat for a number of years. Yet for the sake of my wife and bairns at home I had to submit to very unpleasant orders many a time. It was only when we were working with ropes and blocks that we were able to hold our own with other men.

The older of my two brothers in law, John Purves, only stayed three months in the USA. His wife had all her luggage packed ready to leave home to join her husband that day he arrived back in Eyemouth. He never sent word that he was coming home he just walked into his home and said to his dear wife 'This is me, what do you think of me.'

The poor wife couldn't find her voice for sometime, and at last she said 'Is that you John?'

'Aye,' he said, 'its me, whay dae yea think it is?'

'But,' said his dear wife 'where hey yea come fray?'

'Where dae yea think' said John.

'Weel,' said his wife, 'I am ready to go to America.'

'Weel,' said John 'Yea can gang if ye like, but am hame and I will bide at hame.'

And John stayed home and never made much more than a livelihood.

His brother Willie returned sometime later to visit but went back to the
U.S.A. and has done well there.

After I had arrived in Trenton I had one pound two shillings and
sixpence after paying my fare and I knew my wife had very little if any
money to maintain her and our children. I sent one pound home so I
had two shillings and sixpence when I started work in Mr Craig's
shipyard and I sent home one pound each week. I intended to go
sailing on the lake steamers whenever navigation opened, but after
nine months in Trenton Mr Craig took me down to his new shipyard
at Toledo.

The day we left Trenton he said 'James you take one shift of clothes, a
brace and bit, a spike mall and a block and tackle. Go to the railway
station and I will meet you there.'

I went as ordered but Mr Craig could not be found there. The train
was near due. I heard her whistle and I was wondering what I should do.
I saw her come round the bend and stop and then Mr Craig got onboard.
Of course I didn't know that it was customary for folk to be able to stop
trains out of the station in America.

On our way to Toledo I learnt from Mr Craig the secret of his success
in life.

It was evening when we arrived in Toledo and we had some miles to
walk to the new shipyard. Mr Craig shouldered the block and tackle and
off we went. When about half way there, Judge Collins passed us with
his horse and buggy. He asked Mr Craig to get up beside him and
relieved me of most of my burden, which made it easier for me. When
we arrived at the shipyard Mr Craig showed me the work he wanted
done.

Then he said 'Now James all the material which comes into this
shipyard will be under your charge. There will soon be row boats coming
round here after dark and I want you to order all the men off them at
once'.

'If they refuse', I said, 'What then.'

Mr Craig replied 'If these men refuse to leave, drop one of the big
stones through their boat'.

'Well,' I said, 'that means trouble and most likely there will be two
men in each boat and I see that each man here carries a revolver.'

Mr Craig said that was true and he then handed me a six-chamber
revolver and also a large pistol and said 'Don't let anyone get you first.'

I said to him 'suppose I hurt or kill any of these men who come prowling round here after dark what then?'

He said 'use your good judgement, but if you do get into difficulty I will stand by you.'

'Now then James' he said, 'We must find board and lodgings for you.'

There was a house inside the shipyard but Mr Craig had let a family into that house until their new home was ready for them. So we went and saw Mrs Applegate. Mr Craig said to her 'Will you take this man to lodge and board with you?' But she said 'No he will not come in here.'

Then we went down to Ironville, a village one and half miles further down the Maumee river but we had no better luck there. By then it was getting dark and starting to rain.

Mr Craig said, 'Now James we will go back to shipyard' and this we did. Mrs Applegate was very surprised to see us again but Mr Craig said 'Now Mrs there is one of two things you must do'.

'And what must I do?' she said.

'You must take this man to board with you or you must leave this house at once. Choose now which you will do.' And she bade me come in. And for a little while things were not like they are in paradise but we learned to like each other and I have paid that family many friendly visits and helped them out of their troubles more than once.

The first night which I spent in the shipyard the rain came down in torrents and continued for a whole week which caused the Johnstown flood in Pennsylvania with a terrible loss of life. I engaged a few men and started work the following week and Mr Craig came to see me every two weeks after that and showed me the work he wanted done. And six months later he and his sons came with their families to live in Toledo and started building iron boats. The shipyard became a busy place and very soon employed over three hundred men.

After six or so months when I worked in Mr Craig's shipyard my wife and family arrived. Mrs Appelgate had moved out of the old house inside the shipyard, so our family were able to move in.

The night watchman at the yard was well advanced in years. Mr Brown was a coloured man and rather nervous, especially on dark nights. But many times he had good cause to be as there were nine large public houses on Front Street opposite the shipyard and the Malleable Iron Works. They were a great black spot on the community and these saloons ruined many fine men who I at one time respected but who soon became slaves to the drink. These men gave the night watchman great trouble. They often stayed in the saloons until late at night and then climbed the fence and took our rowboat to cross the river to their homes on the opposite side.

At these times the watchman came for me which was very annoying. I hated to quarrel with the drunken men. Usually I was on friendly terms with them, yet I could not stand their nasty ways of abusing Mr Brown the night watchman. And they could not have the boats to abandon on the other side of the river at night. Often they would turn ugly and threaten to use force but we never yielded neither to their entreaties or their cursing.

But the crowning day came one Sunday afternoon. Brown came after me in a great hurry. Six men had broken one of the boat's chains and were just leaving the dockside when I arrived. I advised these men to get out of the boat before more trouble arose but they only tried the more to get away. I then leapt onboard the boat. Two or three of the men tried to get hold of me, but I jumped on to the side of boat and then back on to the dock. As they chased me these men, who had been drinking, fell on the side of the boat which then capsized leaving all six of them struggling in the water.

I felt sorry for them and helped them ashore. They were pitiful to look at but very angry and I think they would have thrashed me, yet dared not. I tried to reason with them but of course when drink is in, wit is out and at last the hot air cooled off.

One man who was fine mannered and a kind of favourite with the eighty four men who boarded with Mrs Lafrance in her boarding house had lost his large hand bag when the boat capsized. The bag lay at the bottom of the dock and I fished it up for him. When I dropped it on the dock side the bag burst open and there was a Pay Packet for each man. Most of the boarders had lost part of their belongings earlier that day and not one man ever suspected the thief – but these five men now claimed their own property and the thief ran as fast as possible . . . though under the circumstances his wet clothing hindered his progress.

The men who were angry at me a little while before were now my friends because they had found who had taken their property. And old Mr Brown had peace for sometime afterwards, or at least until six months later.

At midnight that night Mrs Brown came for me in a very agitated state. Three or four men had broken the chain and were twenty yards from the dock in a boat when I got there and were rowing away as fast as possible. I tried to persuade them to bring the boat back to the dock and I thought they might answer me and I might recognise their voice, but they kept quiet and pulled away. My brother-in-law Willie Purves stayed with us and unknown to me he had suspected trouble with these men and had run down to the dock with a Wincheseter rifle which had sixteen bullets. And without saying a word he fired a shot at these men which must have passed through between them, and he was so excited he would have fired again. I pushed the muzzle up in the air and saved the trouble that would have caused!

We then paddled the flat bottomed skiff across the river and found the row boat abandoned, but with no signs of the men. The rifle firing had a quietening effect. Afterwards we had peace in the shipyard at night time and slept well.

But near the saloons was still dangerous – for whenever there was a wedding there was lots of fighting and these men from the Balkan States always used their knives. A murder the same night as a marriage was common, and where we lived, in our new home on the corner of Front and York Street, became a very rough place. However no one ever molested me.

The Malleable Iron Works started and very soon employed five hundred men. Then the flour mill began which very soon put out eleven-hundred barrels of flour each day. Then the oil refinery, the brick and tile factory, the sign factory, all of which were next door to each other, and within two years there were over six hundred dwelling houses, a church, a large public school and all of these buildings seemed to grow up like mushrooms.

My house was the third or fourth which was built in that part of Toledo and that is the reason I became acquainted with so many of the settlers there. Mr Craig built my house for me and I gave him all the money which my wife and I had saved, which was not a large sum, and he didn't charge me any interest for the money which I owed him. And we cleared all the debt on our house within one year from the date we went to live in it. My wife earned good money cleaning the Malleable Iron Works office and I made good money painting new houses and assisting steamers which often grounded coming up the Maumee River and in many other honourable ways which many tradesmen never noticed – or perhaps would not look for. So we were a busy couple all the years we lived in that part of the world.

I worked in Mr Craig's shipyard three years and nine months. I then shipped onboard a cigar boat bound for Duluth. We were loading coal and would have sailed that night but part of the cargo did not come forward that day as expected. The captain said to me at about five that afternoon 'Where do you live?' and I told him it was nearby. He said 'Well you have worked well today and the remainder of our cargo will not be here until morning. You can go home and be here at eleven tomorrow. That will be alright.'

Our second boy Jamie, was less than one week old, having been born in Toledo in 1890 and my wife was not so well as I would have liked her to be. Yet I felt I had to ship on that boat. I was anxious to better our circumstances.

I had some painting to do on my house, so I rose very early next morning to finish it and while busy I heard a whistle blowing while coming down the river. It dawned on me that the Captain had received orders to sail with what quantity of cargo he had onboard and I was right in my judgement. I bade my wife good-bye and ran as fast as I could to the wheeling bridge, intending to leap from the parapet of the bridge and on to the shrouds and make the voyage. But whither for my good or ill I don't know, but the boat passed through the bridge two minutes ahead of me – and all the clothing that I possessed except what I stood in went to the top of Lake Superior.

I rushed to the railway depot to get a train for Detroit, intending to meet my boat passing there. But I was late there also. So I did the next best thing. I went to work in the Malleable Iron Works, much against my will.

Iron Works and Money Troubles

The Iron Works had been established at the same time as the Craig shipyard and most of the employees were Hungarian immigrants or 'Balkan people' as Lough calls them.

Nine months after starting at the Malleable, James was put in charge of all outside work. The man he replaced held an understandable grudge against him and tried to get Lough sacked. This led to an altercation with the overall supervisor Mr Helm during which James held his ground declaring, 'I am an honest man. The Noblest Work of God'.

In spite of his obvious distaste for working at the massive Malleable Iron Works James Lough did as he would do throughout his life – he worked hard, saved hard and succeeded. He could have earned more than he did, but not 'with honour'. He shunned anything that was either illegal or immoral. Honesty was uppermost in Lough's life creed.

Yet the money that James and Maggie grafted to earn was put at risk first by a fire that destroyed the Malleable and then by the great panic of 1893 which led to a run on the banks and great lawlessness in Toledo.

I had never worked inside a building, always in the open. There were ten large furnaces in the melting room where I went to work. I started as a packer, and there were seventeen men on the same job. But they had no sympathy for a stranger. The work was hard and the great heat unbearable. However though I thought I would die yet I kept at the work until I learned how to do it with much more ease. Then I was made leading hand and then foreman over all the outside work.

The foreman in the heating room lived five miles from the work, and on winter nights when snow was falling he often coaxed me to take his place to see the furnaces charged, which was a very particular job. Each furnace held a certain number of pots filled with articles, and every pot had to be placed exactly or else some furnace would go out. And it was my duty to see that the full number of pots were placed in each furnace. The charge men were all foreigners and very vicious when crossed and when the furnaces were not properly filled I had to order these men to take out every pot and start to fill the furnaces properly. These men were not pleasant to be near at these times. But I saw that they respected me. I was with them very often till near midnight — many times against my own wishes but no one ever molested me.

After I had worked nine months in the heating room I was offered the foreman's job over all outside work.

The plant stood on fourteen acres. We often had steamers which would bring cargoes of twelve hundred tons of pig-iron. There were eleven different grades of iron and each grade had to be piled up by itself and I often had twenty-five or thirty men to look after as this job was done. And the man who was foreman previous to me was one of their own countrymen and a favourite with the manager of the moulding shop who had shares in the works. This manager was a big strong man who I thought did not like me very much. So I expected to have trouble before many weeks expired. My reason for thinking so was the man who was foreman previous to me still worked as a labourer and often watched the way I did the work. He and Mr Helm, the manager of the moulding shops, were often together and I had the idea that trouble was brewing for me. And I hadn't long to wait.

I had my men working in the coal sheds when the man who had my job before I got it came for me, saying, 'Mr Helm wants you at once Jamie'. And he said, 'Mr Helm will give you more than you want today,' and I saw Tommy was gloating over what he thought would be my downfall.

But my Scotch blood leapt in my veins and at that moment I could not help looking at Tommy with scorn, and yet I pitied him and I said 'Well Tommy. Go back and tell your master that I am here at work if he wants me.' And Tommy told him just what I said, and after some minutes later I heard Mr Helm calling. Then he whistled a few times, but I never turned round until he came right up to me and said 'Didn't you hear me calling on you Jamie?'

I turned round and said, 'Were you calling me Mr Helm?'

He said 'Yes, didn't you hear me?'

'I did hear you, but I don't answer anyone who calls as you did. That is the way we call on our dogs in Scotland and believe me, Mr Helm, I want you to know that I am not a dog. I am an honest man. The noblest work of God'.

The storm in Mr Helm's breast had spent itself. He looked me up and down for a minute and then said, 'The pig iron is mixed. Will you come with me and try to explain how it happened?' I said 'Yes, I will go with you with pleasure.' And sure enough in the middle of one pile there were eight or ten bars of a different grade.

Mr Helm asked if I could explain how that had happened.

I said, 'I can. And if you will walk with me I will show you where these bars have been carried from.' Mr Helm said to me 'You are quite right. Now, tell me how do you think these bars happened to be mixed?' I said 'You know, Mr Helm, I have one or two friends here who don't care for me, and while I have been home for dinner one or two of these poor friends intended to get me into trouble. They carried these bars from this lot, and placed these bars where you found them'.

Mr Helm said, 'I understand. And these few bars would have spoiled the whole furnace of iron'. And from that day Mr Helm became my intimate friend.

All went well with me and I worked lots of overtime. There were six melting furnaces in these works and each had a chimney made of iron over one hundred feet high and nine feet in diameter. I had painted these chimneys several times. The managers thought they had too much draught and asked for tenders from contractors to cut twenty feet off the top of each chimney. The contractors counted on building scaffolding right to the top of each chimney, which would cost a lot of money. Much more than they expected to have to pay. The managers – through Mr Helm – asked me if I could do the work, and after some conversation I agreed that I could.

The managers were very pleased and asked how much material I wanted. I said one pole twelve feet long with iron pins at each end and also a block and tackle. 'How much scaffolding' they said, and I said, 'None.' They then asked me how many men I wanted, and I said, 'One.' And these men looked at each other and shook their heads.

It seemed to me the managers thought the contractors' price much too high; my price much too low for their liking. So two days passed before I heard anything from them. But then the superintendent asked me to start and said I was to order whatever I wanted. With two helpers I cut twenty feet off each long chimney and afterwards rounded off each chimney. I was paid a nice little sum for my work.

My wife and I worked hand in hand and saved quite a nice sum of money. Too much to keep in our home to be safe. So I informed the manager in the office that I would not come to work on Saturday as I had business to attend to. Mr Lewis tried to advise me that I should come to work, seeing as we were so busy and my thirty men would not manage well without me. Mr Lewis, who was also our Sunday school super-intendent, offered to do my business in the city for me.

I told Mr Lewis I wanted to put some money in the bank and he said, 'I am going to the bank today, can you trust me to bank your money for you?' I agreed to give him all of our money, which I did, and I saw him put the money in the drawers of his desk, and I then went to work.

My wife cleaned the Malleable Iron Works office as usual and I carried hot water to my wife to help her, and that Saturday night before leaving the office she asked me time and again, 'Did you see Mr Lewis put our money in his desk?' I replied with some emphasis that I did, something which I have often regretted saying. 'Well' she said, 'I am sure something will happen. We will lose our money'.

The reason she felt so uncomfortable was that I had seen Mr Lewis that same afternoon and he had said to me, 'I am sorry Mr Lough, but I did not get to the bank as I expected today, and I was afraid to trust your money with anyone else, but I will certainly bank your money on Monday.' And because our hard earned money was in that office my wife hesitated for some time to close the door. She had a kind of premonition that something would happen, and we would lose what we had toiled so hard to get. And I could not persuade her otherwise.

It was near midnight when we arrived at our home, and at ten minutes to four on Sunday morning I awoke out of a deep sleep. Our bedroom was lighted up with a strange red glow. I was wondering what was the cause. Then someone called 'The Malleable is on fire!'

I hurried part of my clothes on, my wife reminding me all the time of her presentment the previous night. I met the night watchman at the office gate and the next moment the high wall collapsed and fell close at our heels as we ran for our lives.

We called on the manager who lived a little way from the works, which were now a terrible blaze. The heating room was six hundred and eighteen feet long, and the large office was in the front of that and both these places made a huge bonfire. The Superintendent told me to go home and put more clothes and an overcoat on and there I met my wife who was almost collapsing. I tried my best to cheer her up while at the same moment my heart was nearly down in my boots.

I was put on watch at once with orders not to allow any persons to enter the ruins and was on duty all Sunday night, through Monday night until Tuesday. My wife brought me something to eat at meal hour and each time she came I knew the first words she would say. 'Have you seen Mr Lewis? Did he tell you about our money?' These words were ever ready on her tongue and no wonder – for she had worked very hard for the money which I saw him put in his drawer. And if he left it there then we knew its fate, and the suspense became like a cancer worm eating out our Peace of Mind.

It is often much better to know even the worst.

Of course I had seen Mr Lewis very often during those three days but I knew he was worrying terribly regarding our money and I could not mention the matter to him. But on Tuesday I noticed his countenance had changed for the better and when he spoke I saw the friendly tear trickle down his cheek and he clasped my hand and said, 'Oh Mr Lough! I have good news for you. Your money is safe.'

I need hardly say that it was a great relief. Mr Lewis said 'On Saturday night I put your money into the safe which twisted and burnt like a cinder in the fire. But if you only knew the joy which filled my heart when I pulled your money out of that safe!' He said that 'All day Sunday and Monday, every time I looked at you, my heart yearned but your smile sent me away wondering how you managed.'

The strange thing to me is that I didn't know I was smiling to him. But I could not stay any longer on watch. I had to run home with the good news to my wife.

And after a while the Malleable was rebuilt and everyone was busy again. I worked many long hours and we saved all we could with honour. I saw several ways we could have made more money than we did, but these ways would have interrupted our Peace of Mind so we left those ways alone. But each pay day increased our little stock in First National Bank until the great Pullman strike started and very soon every work in the country closed down.

I had been the last man to start work in the heating room and of course I fully expected to be the first man to be paid off. And every evening when I came home my wife always said, 'Well, are you discharged then?' But I was kept working there all during the strike.

The engineman and the night-watchman and myself were the only men kept at work. And the manager sent word to me saying that if I ran out of jobs to do I must not stay at home but come to the office and they would find work for me. And I made more money during the strike than at any other time while I was in the U.S.A.

The strike spread over the whole country until every works closed down, and hundreds of idle, desperate men stood outside the entrance of our works and no man or woman were safe who had five dollars in his possession. And each pay day I fully expected to be held up, but no one ever molested me, and I passed through the crowd and home with my wages to my wife.

Perhaps the reason these men did let me past with my two week's wages was that our children were all young and I needed all that I earned. Of course, I knew and was friendly with all of these men, but lots of banks failed every week, houses were broken into and robbed and many murders committed. I had a six chamber revolver under my pillow and also a large pistol and a large chopping axe at my bedside each night. All doors and windows were barricaded and under these conditions we did not sleep sound. These precautions would not have prevented desperate men from entering our home, but would have meant a greater loss of life.

But when things were at their worst my wife became very anxious regarding our money in the bank. She advised me every day to stop work and get our money home in case the bank failed. So I brought our money from the bank and it was only when we had it home that we realised the dangers. We could not make up our minds where to hide the money. At first we intended removing a board off the wainscoating round our kitchen; then we thought if these money-hunters came in they would notice the board had been removed and would soon find the money.

Then we lifted our floor cloth and spread the dollars on our kitchen floor, then re-laid the floor cloth carefully. And after that we were careful where we put our feet down. We didn't want to crush the precious bits of paper.

What a life that was for us who had worked like slaves and had got the stuff which had enticed us to leave our home and friends and all we counted dear. And now we were tramping it under our feet. We sometimes thought we were fools for saving it. We should have done like many others and had a good time and spent the money. If we had we would not have been in such danger at that time. But we knew its value because it had cost us so much to get it.

And while we were worrying over the dangers of losing both the money and our lives, our friend Mr Craig, who was also a director of the First National Bank, came to our home and said 'Now Maggie, whatever made you lift the money out of the bank?' Maggie replied we were afraid that the bank would fail and we would lose all of it.

'Have you got it safe Maggie?' He said. 'No matter where you hide it if these men come they will find it. Even if you put it behind your wainscoating or under your floor cloth they will find the money and if you or James tries to stop them you will loose your own lives.' And at that moment Mr Craig was standing right on top of the money.

When I came home from work she told me what Mr Craig had said and we racked our brains just to know a safe place where to hide our earthly treasures where no thieves could break through and steal it. And at last we settled on our chicken house which stood about seventy feet back from our house.

We put the money in a stone jar and pulled two boards off the floor of our chicken house and put the jar and dollars down, then fastened the boards and tried to feel happy because our hidden treasure was safe with our chickens on the watch. We hardly expected them to hatch young ones, but they did.

One evening about three months later, after my hard day's work was over, I read the newspaper while supper was being prepared. I called on my wife to listen as I read a statement regarding stolen money, which a man had hid in a metal pot and put in a hole which the man had dug in his garden. He put the pot with the money in the hole and covered it up; thinking it would be safe. But when the man wanted the stolen money he found the dampness had done its deadly work and the money was all eaten away.

At that my wife started to run to our chicken house. I could hardly persuade her to wait until darkness came, but daylight seemed to linger much longer than ever before. We were both praying in our hearts for darkness to come quickly, but my wife could not wait until then so we crept out and lifted the boards off the floor of the chicken house and brought the jar with contents into our kitchen. We had to break the jar and to our horror there lay our earthly treasure . . . But very many of the paper dollars we dared not touch – moths had eaten thousands of holes in them.

We had no supper that night. We didn't know what to do for the best, for we dared not handle lots of that money which we had struggled so hard to gather up. The moths and rust had corrupted the once precious treasure and it seemed of little or no use to us.

But just when our hearts seemed almost to fail us it seemed strange, for our faithful friend Mr Craig came to our rescue – and we were right glad to see him. He noted the numbers on each dollar and the bank helped us a lot. We then ran large bills for groceries and lots of other necessities, then we bought a piece of ground and paid for it with lots of the damaged money so after a while we got rid of the filthy lucre which had given us so much trouble and worry. It had cost us so much hard work to get the rubbish and it spoiled our happiness while we tried to keep it safe. Then we had great trouble to get rid of it honestly, so it must be the root of all evil.

But after a while we forgot all about these troubles. The great Pullman strike was now over and we were busy as man and wife saving enough to pay our own way and something for old age coming on us.

Back Home to be Master at Last

Although there is little doubt that James Lough would have been content to stay in the United States and become a thorough American, his beloved wife Maggie Purves was not. True to her promise she left for home exactly five years after arriving in Toledo. James, hopeful that Maggie might change her mind, remained in Ohio. If she did not return he intended to sell up their home and follow on some months later.

Disaster nearly befell the family when the ship Maggie and the children were sailing in struck an iceberg in mid-Atlantic. James felt his wife come to him at that moment as he lay, fever-stricken, in bed in Toledo. His family survived the raging seas and Lough, knowing how close he had come to losing all that he truly held dear, bade America farewell.

As had been the case when he first arrived in the United States and when his brother-in-law John Purves had gone home to Eyemouth, James Lough sent no word ahead of his intentions. He arrived on the very day that his son George was born – brought to their home by 'Tam Stane', which is the name of a rocky outcrop in the bay. Tam Stane is Eyemouth's own version of the Stork.

James and Maggie had left a batch of unpaid bills when they flitted to America. They returned with enough money to settle these in full, purchase the house at number seventeen George Street for £250, and buy both a fishing boat and a small trading sloop. But James did not wish to return to the sea as a fisherman. He wanted to do on the Scottish east coast what he had failed to manage on the North American Great Lakes. He wanted to go into business as a coastal trader with his own fleet of ships.

We started kippering herring, which I am certain would have paid us extra well but my wife could not make up her mind to stop many years more in U.S.A. and since I was earning good wages at my work, we didn't put our best into the kippering business.

After five years stay my wife and children left Toledo and she was not certain whether she would return or not. I went to New York with her and our children and saw them onboard the *SS Ethiopia*. I watched until they were out of sight.

My heart was sad. I had often left them. But that was the first time they had left me.

I boarded my train for Toledo. I was very tired and slept a little but caught a chill and sore throat which got worse each day as I was at work. On Sunday I fell ill and returned to bed during the afternoon.

And I had a strange experience. It was impossible for me to sleep as my throat troubled me. So I had turned my face to the wall; I lay on my right side; my hand was on top of the bed covers. I saw my wife look over my left shoulder as plainly as ever I did and I even felt her warm breath on the back of my hand. I turned round to speak to her. I looked at the clock. It was twenty-five minutes to four pm and I could not forget that strange presentiment. And I learned afterwards that was the exact time when the *SS Ethiopia* struck an iceberg.

The steamer ran on to the submerged part of the iceberg which smashed her bows against the part high out of the water. It then heeled over on her beam-ends and slid down off the submerged part. The ship began to fill very quickly with water. It was then my wife said to our children 'What will your father think when he hears the news that we are all at the bottom of the sea?'

So Spirit acts on Spirit. It was at that moment that Maggie – my dear wife – came so near to me on that Sunday afternoon.

It may seem strange and hard for some folks to believe but it is true. When the *Ethiopia* began to sink the Captain ordered every boat to be lowered and all women and children first into the boats. Our oldest boy Robert was fifteen years old and my wife refused to go into the lifeboat and leave her boy. She and all our children decided to stay on the steamer and our children went on their knees, near their mother and prayed with all the earnestness their young hearts could command. I am convinced the Lord heard and answered their prayers.

The Captain ordered everyone to man the pumps. Then every available man, both crew and passengers were ordered to carry bags of flour from the after hold to fill the fore peak where the steamer was badly damaged. Then the men removed the cargo from the forehold to the after hold and that raised the steamer's beam out of the water quite a bit. The steamer lay four days during these operations and the weather kept fine all the while. The ship then proceeded across the Atlantic contrary to the crew and passengers' expectations.

After sixteen days the *Ethiopia* steamed up the Clyde to Glasgow. There were great rejoicings that day, and no man was so glad as the writer when I received a telegram from the owners that all mine were landed safe. I have often wondered if anyone could ever understand what harm the suspense did to me those terrible days.

My wife and children had a warm welcome when they arrived back in Eyemouth.

That experience with the iceberg caused my wife to make her mind up not to return to U.S.A.

I worked nine months after my wife and children went home but I realised life was too short to live in that fashion and I informed my employers of my intention to leave the U.S.A. The Superintendent, Mr Helm, walked quite a way up the road with me and advised me not to stay long in Scotland, and that if I would come back to work in the Malleable Iron Works the company would do their best for me. I thanked Mr Hopkins and Mr Booth, two of the managers of the Malleable, and also my dear friends Mr and Mrs Craig for all their kindness to me.

I intended to work my passage across the Atlantic but I learned I could purchase a ticket for the small sum of two pounds ten shillings from New York to Glasgow. I bought my ticket and shipped on the *City of New York*. We landed at Southampton and then by train to London and on to Glasgow. I then arrived at Edinburgh and got the first train that morning and had no time to purchase a ticket until I reached Dunbar. While coming along the coastline that morning I saw the fishing fleet going out to sea, which thrilled my soul more than I can tell.

I had not sent any word to my folks. I just wanted to give them a surprise, but I found our house empty. It was washing day and my wife had taken her washing out to dry and our children were at school, and Mr Craig's Aunt Sarah was the only person in our house.

I met several folks on my way from the railway station but none of them knew me, so Aunt Sarah entertained me until my wife came home. Then my father and mother – Robert Lough and Agnes Windram – came and were delighted to see me after seven years and nine months absence. Our home was soon filled with friends.

That was a great night in our family experience for Doctor Forsyth paid a visit to that famous place Tam Stane where all the bairns in

Eyemouth come from, and that night our third boy, George, was born – 1895, November 22.

And next morning our home was very cheerful indeed. Mr Craig's Aunt Sarah was very anxious to make me comfortable and tried her best to nurse my dear wife but the work proved too hard for her and she was taken sick.

Then I found enough work which kept me busy for several weeks. I had to nurse my wife and also Aunt Sarah and staying indoors didn't agree well with me. I started to look around for a ship and while on the train to Berwick, Mr Munro the old Kirk minister came beside me and during our conversation he asked me what I intended to do for my living. I told him I intended to buy a ship and go into the coasting trade. 'Well,' he said, 'You will go in my ship the *Fiery Cross.*' I said 'Tell me what my pay will be?' And I also said, 'Do you expect me to go deck hand?' And he said 'Yes, for a little while,' but then he added 'My captain and mate are not well acquainted with the Scottish coast and you will very soon be in charge of the *Fiery Cross.*'

I said 'Mr Munro, you will excuse me but I will not stoop to do such low work. I shall never do any man out of his job.' And Mr Munro became my opponent from that day.

I heard of a ship near the size I wanted. She had been caught in a storm and lost all her sails and needed a whole new outfit and it may seem strange, but the price the owner wanted for that ship was the very sum which I possessed. The owner asked me home with him, then to a prayer meeting and I heard him pray and I thought I was dealing with an honest man and I trusted him. But before I finished my first voyage I found I had been deceived. However I was determined not to look back.

I had made ready to sail along with four other ships bound to Hartlepool, but none of them sailed. The captains thought the weather too risky. However I did sail and arrived at Hartlepool an entire stranger. I wanted a cargo of good house coal, yet I had no money to pay for the cargo. There were several coal exporters in Hartlepool but Leonard and Danby's name appealed to me and I called at their office, told them of my circumstances and asked them to load me a cargo which I promised to pay at the end of the month. These kind men trusted me and loaded my first cargo. The weather was stormy and none of the ships which were ready to sail when I sailed had arrived, and now a heavy NE storm was raging amidst mountains of sea.

Leonard and Danby asked me to take my first cargo to Whitby. They had a large business there which had no coal. I agreed at once because these men had so readily obliged me. Next morning the sea was down a lot, and I sailed along with a very large fleet of vessels, bound to many different ports. The storm seemed finished but after midday I noticed signs of a renewal and in a little while the storm burst with great fury and the sea rose very quickly. Whitby harbour is open to NE seas and I was aware of the danger of entering that harbour.

My ship was not insured and I had spent every penny which I possessed on it and I was much afraid I would lose the *Achilles* that same evening. When crossing the harbour bar some heavy seas threatened to swamp our heavy-laden vessel and I was very much relieved when we passed inside the piers. All the ships that were ready to sail when I left port were still moored at the buoys.

I had beat them on my first voyage and I sailed the same day as these vessels but on my second voyage.

I loaded at Hartlepool a cargo of house coal and arrived home and advertised the cargo at seventeen shillings and sixpence per ton and sold all the cargo out of the ship. I then loaded a cargo of potatoes for Sunderland, which I discharged to Mr Maw, potato merchant who treated me kindly.

I then saw Messrs Harty, coal exporters, and asked them to load my ship with the best house coal for home. I told them I would pay for the cargo at the end of one month, but they were cautious men and wanted time to consider. I could not blame them for this. As I left their office a tall smartly dressed fellow passed me, turned around and asked if I were master of the *Achilles*.

I said that I was and he said, 'What are you going to do now?'

I told him that I wanted a cargo of good house coal to sell at my home, but that I could not pay ready cash and at once he said, 'I will load you a cargo'.

I said, 'When will you load?' He replied 'Get your ship up to the Hetton coal drop and I will load you tomorrow.'

I said 'Would you not like to hear something about me first?' But he said, 'Oh no'. I said, 'You are rather kind for my liking.' But he replied 'You get your ship up to Hetton and you will get a load tomorrow'.

Of course I was anxious to get the cargo, so the next day my ship was at Hetton ready and waiting for orders to load. But no orders came until the fifth day of waiting. And it was then that I realised that I was correct in thinking Mr John Soppat's offer to load was not sincere. For while we waited at Hetton Drops, he was communicating to a merchant in Eyemouth who happened to be my intimate friend – but Mr Soppat didn't know that until sometime later.

However we did manage to get a load of coal and sailed for home where we sold half the cargo out of the ship and had great difficulty to find a shed to store the other half. I then sailed again for Sunderland and loaded a half cargo of lime and a half cargo of coal for a merchant in Dornoch.

We discharged the coal first while a strong west wind was blowing along. We had a very rough passage from Sunderland and my old ship had been leaking while on our voyage. The water had run down the side of the mizzenmast. After our day's work was done and with only the half cargo of lime to discharge the next day we were enjoying ourselves at sea, when we were surprised by a fire in our hold.

Our ship was on fire and with no help near, all the men being at home at Dornoch which was three miles distant from the little ferry where we were discharging. We had to leave our ship and we lay among the whin bushes all night, and were very glad to see the men who came to discharge the lime the next morning.

Our mizzenmast and the supports were still burning, and the men only worked one hour and could not suffer the stench caused by the burning timbers any longer. I was at my wits end as to how to quench the fire. We dared not throw water on to the fire, and I offered the men double pay if they would work the cargo out. They agreed but had to stop again. Then I engaged men to bring sand which was plentiful near by, and after some desperate efforts we kept the fire under control and finished discharging. We cut our mizzenmast three feet below the deck which kept the fire from reaching the deck and saved the ship.

After repairs were finished I wired Mr Soppat 'Sailing today for Sunderland. Have cargo ready.' On arrival at Sunderland Mr Soppat informed me that I would have to wait twelve days to get a load. That was very mean of him to get me to come that long journey and then to tell me I couldn't get a load for twelve days. My ship was moored up the river at Hetton docks and after waiting two days Mr Soppat offered to load if I would pay the expense of towing and the dock dues and two shillings and sixpence per ton more for coals – but I could not agree to this.

I had occasion to go to Hetton coal office and Mr Laing the manager said to me 'What are you going to do now?' I told him what Mr Soppat had offered me, and Mr Laing advised me what to do. He became my friend that very day twenty-four years ago, and Father Time has cemented us in closer friendship, which I hope will never be broken.

Mr Laing said to me, 'Go and offer Mr Soppat so much per ton for a cargo of coals to be loaded in the dock, and if accepts your offer then load. But if he refuses your offer then come here and we will load your ship direct from the colliery. Mr Soppat is a good customer to us and he gives me very many presents. But he has robbed you and I cannot stand him any longer.'

I did as Mr Laing advised me to do, but Mr Soppat refused my offer. At that time I owed him eighteen pounds and I promised to send him the money. I knew one or two men who owned little ships like mine and who were sent to the Poor House through Mr Soppat and I was careful not to accept the offer he made to me.

A few years later I had two steamers running to Sunderland and when near ready to discharge a cargo of 'generals' Mr Soppat came asking me to give him a job checking our cargo. He was very shabbily dressed, his boots were entirely done, he looked hungry and I agreed for which he seemed very thankful.

I lost my old sailing ship *Achilles* at Newbiggin on the Northumberland Coast. The ship needed more money for repairs than I cared to spend on her, so I sold her as she lay on the rocks.

At that time my oldest son Robert was determined to go to sea, and I advised him to learn to be an engineer, as I saw plainly the days of sailing ships were done. I had saved two hundred pounds during the two years I had sailed the old ship and I told my son if he became a good engineer I would try my best to have a steamer ready when he finished his apprenticeship. In the meantime I went back to fishing and did well, and then sold my fishing boat and fishing gear when my son finished his time as an apprentice with John Cran and Somerville, Leith.

I had a new steamer ready, but I needed fifty pounds to pay the builder the amount which I had promised – and there was no one I could borrow that amount from. I had asked one man who said he was sorry but he could not oblige me. The same man offered to loan me three-hundred-and-fifty pounds one year later. By then I was doing well and did not require any help.

But I must mention the struggle that I had to get my first steamer. I had saved near five hundred pounds and with my son went to Paton and Hendry's office at Glasgow. They had a lot of small steamers just like the size I was looking for. The manager had one eight years old, priced at sixteen-hundred-pounds and he pressed me to purchase it. But after considering I refused and I later found I had done the wise thing, for it cost eight-hundred-pounds to repair the same steamer not three months later for wear and tear. That would have been serious for me.

However we called on Mr Marshall of Maryhill, Glasgow and I told him how much money I had, that my son was a practical engineer and that if he could give me a steamer like the one he had just launched, and if he had her ready near the beginning or middle of May, I was sure to get fifteen cargoes of salt to run.

After hearing my story the builder surprised me by saying 'If you are telling the truth, I will build you a steamer.' I said 'That is good, but what about the outfit?' And Mr Marshall said, 'I will furnish an engine and boiler, a steam winch and everything in the latest modern style, and I will take what money you have to pay down. I will draw up a bill for three years and if you cannot pay the bill off at the end of three years, we will renew the bill.'

So said, I signed the contract and the steamer, the *SS Maggie Purves* was built – but not until three months later than the contract called for, and on that account I lost the fifteen cargoes of salt, and a lot of other cargoes besides.

But after I became acquainted with the merchants I found enough cargoes to keep the steamer busy, and the builder was fully paid before the bill became due.

We then saved money quickly and in 1908 I ordered another steamer, the *SS Maggie Lough* which carried one-hundred-and-eighty tons cargo and twenty tons bunkers. A splendid sea boat which paid us well. I had gone seventeen-hundred and eighty pounds in debt for the *SS Maggie Lough* and in 1912 both steamers were clear of debt.

SS Maggie Lough was running three cargoes per week to Aberdeen, and one day started discharging at seven in the morning and did not finish until four-thirty pm. The ship then loaded a cargo of cement the same evening and sailed at nine pm, arriving at its destination the next morning.

We certainly earned all the money which we received – and many times finished a voyage when other steamers were running for shelter. We often entered the dock at Burntisland and also at Grangemouth two hours before the high water, loaded cargo and bunkers and sailed at sharp high water, so being only two hours in port. Many shipbrokers wondered how I found cargoes to keep both steamers running steady and also sail myself as master of the SS *Maggie Lough*.

These two steamers cleared over twenty-thousand pounds and they are good boats yet, and if managed well will work for lots of money.

But it is the men who run the boats and not the boats who run the men.

The Great War and More Sorrow Besides . . .

*The coastal trading business boomed and James and three of his four sons –
Robert, Jamie and later John – established themselves as keen merchants able
to sail in and out of ports from Shetland to South Shields. In his memoirs
James refers to his eldest son Robert as 'the engineer' while his youngest boy
John is the 'mate'.*

*The coming of the Great War changed everything. In 1915 the SS Maggie
Lough was commandeered as a supply ship by the Royal Navy, but as early as
August 1914 James's boys were involved with the enemy when they reported
being boarded by German submariners in the Firth of Forth. Days later, on
September 5th 1914, HMS Pathfinder was sunk in the Firth after being hit
by a torpedo. Almost three hundred men were drowned.*

*Lough and his sons spent the duration of the war ferrying supplies to the
Grand Fleet at Scapa Flow. It was hard, harsh and dangerous work and
James is sometimes scathing about the naval officials, especially those involved
in catering and stores, who treated him with disdain. He writes of being
ordered to venture to an outlying island during a 'dead lee shore' when strong
winds were blowing from the sea to the land, making navigation treacherous
if not downright impossible. The officer who delivered the order apparently
had no idea what a dead lee shore was.*

*War service ruined the health of James's three seafaring boys and led each to
an early grave. The youngest, John Purves Lough, who had been born in 1900,
died in 1923. The eldest, Robert Lough, born in 1880, died the following year.
Jamie, the only American in the family who had been born in Toledo in 1893,
died from the same mysterious illness as his brothers in 1929, aged just thirty-six.
That left George, the only boy not to have gone to sea, as the sole surviving son.*

*James's beloved wife did not live to see her boys suffer. Maggie Purves died
in May 1918 at the age of sixty-two.*

All went well with us until the Admiralty commandeered our boats in
1915 and the *SS Maggie Lough* was sent to Scapa Flow. I then sold *SS
Maggie Purves*.

SS Maggie Lough was attached to the Grand Fleet. And I received a certificate from the Director of Transports stating that though they loaded *SS Maggie Lough* and though they put a pilot on board, yet I was responsible – and while I could be ordered to go anywhere, if I considered it not prudent then I need not go.

Just a few months before we were ordered to Scapa Flow the *SS Maggie Lough* left Grangemouth with a cargo of coal bound for Stonehaven. No steamers were allowed to be underway in the Firth of Forth after dark, so the *SS Maggie Lough* was anchored in Largo Bay. After supper my son Robert, the engineer, had first watch.

Once the fires were banked up the engineer was on deck leaning against the engine-room casing having a smoke when he heard a man's voice. He wondered where it came from. The crew were all asleep. The engineer stepped from the casing, intending to go to the forecastle to enquire if one of the crew had been talking. As the engineer stepped out from the casing two men sprang over the bulwark, their faces almost came against our engineer's face. One of these men spoke in English, saying 'Hello. Where are you from? Where are you bound to? What is your cargo?'

These were the questions our destroyer's officers always asked and, of course, our engineer was off his guard and answered the questions. The man said, 'Well, I must see your cargo.'

The engineer replied that would cause trouble as the crew were asleep, and the hatches all battered down. 'But,' said the engineer, 'I will let you see our bills of loading.'

'That will do,' said the stranger, 'let me see your bills of loading.'

'Come down below where there is light' said our engineer.

'Show us the way,' said the intruder.

My son still thought these men were from one of the destroyers who were guarding our coast at that time. But when our engineer was going down the hold he saw one man pull his revolver out of his pocket and motion to his companion to do the same. Our engineer wondered to see that, but both men came down while he was getting the papers ready.

The stranger said, 'What town are you anchored off?'

'Methil.'

'And where is Leven?' he asked.

'That is Leven over there,' gestured the engineer.

'How can that be?' said the stranger 'You have just told us that is Methil'.

Our engineer looked hard at him and said 'I gave you our bills of loading and you haven't looked at them. Tell me who gave you authority to come aboard here? What ship are you from?'

The stranger evaded the questions, but my son said 'Tell me what ship are you from and who gave you authority to come on board here?'

The intruder said, 'If we are from a German ship, what would you do?'

My son, the engineer, replied 'We are only merchantmen and not prepared to do much, but I don't think you have any right to come here. You better hand back those bills of loading.' And this they did without looking at them.

These men still held their revolvers in their hand and again asked, 'What would you do if we are from a German ship?'

At that moment our mate, my other son John, who had awoken out of his sleep and had heard the intruders say, 'What would you do if we are from a German ship?' shouted up 'Oh, we would shoot you.'

The intruder put his revolver under our mate's chin which sent a shiver through him. Our mate apologised, saying he was not fully awake and told the intruder that he did not mean what he had just said. That it was only a little joke. The intruder then handed our engineer the bills of loading without having looked at them and asked him to come on deck. He then said to our engineer, 'Now, show me which is Leven and tell me, is there a sandy beach at Leven?'

'Don't tell anyone about this visit,' said the intruder. 'We are wanting some oil'. And with that the two men got into their collapsible boat and disappeared into the darkness.

I was at home doing repairs to the *SS Maggie Purves* at that time, and I reported the case to the authorities and as a consequence the Firth of Forth was closed two days later.

I had arranged for the *SS Maggie Lough* to load cement slabs at Aberdeen for Methil and I had some difficulty to persuade the Admiralty to allow the steamer to enter Methil. And on the voyage to Methil our crew sighted a submarine periscope near Fifeness, and reported the same to the coastguard here. He thought it might be a British submarine doing practice. But on the Saturday our first British government ship *Pathfinder* was sunk with great loss of life.

Our coastguard had been mistaken. He worried himself so much owing to his mistake that he became seriously ill and died.

While at Scapa Flow we had many exciting experiences. The mine layer *Abdele* had layed ninety-four mines which had broken adrift and we were sent to search for them. The navigating officer who had been in charge when laying the mines came along with twenty-five men on board the SS *Maggie Lough*.

We only got three mines during that forenoon and when the officer and men went onboard their boat for dinner, the officer said 'Perhaps we will have better luck this afternoon.'

I said 'I don't know what better luck we could expect', and he looked hard at me and said 'We have only got three mines.'

I said 'Yes, but we found the mines very quick. The delay was in getting them on board. You must surely know the cause of the delay?'

But he said 'No, I do not. And I want you to take full charge this afternoon'.

I refused, but he insisted and when he came on board after dinner he said to me 'You say now what you want us to do.' And we got fourteen mines that afternoon. Later the commander again came on board SS *Maggie Lough* and gave me great credit for the way I had handled our steamer and the way I had found the mines. He stated that we had saved the Admiralty thirteen thousand pounds that day and he tried his best to get us to stand by him all during the war. But after we had found forty-seven of the ninety-four mines which were adrift we were sent to other work.

Several times during our service we had no food for two or three days during stormy weather. If we were a few minutes late in coming alongside the parent ship and finding the canteen closed and there being no food for us to eat, we had to find anchorage for the night and go supperless to bed. I sometimes quarrelled with the naval stores officer because of his wrong orders and yet he always spoke to me when passing.

Once we loaded a full cargo of door frames and windows and building materials for listening stations on outlying islands. It was blowing a heavy gale and no boat dared to go near those islands until the sea had run smooth. But the N.S.O (naval stores officer) ordered us away at once. So I left the boat in the charge of our mate while I intervened with the N.S.O.

His desk stood opposite the office door and as soon as I opened the door he looked at me with a scowl on his face. He said, 'Are you not away yet skipper?'

'Not yet' I replied. 'Why not?' said he.

'Don't you consider the elements?' I said.

'What have the elements got to do with it? Don't you know the men are waiting on your cargo?'

'That may be true' I said 'But do you really want me to go on that island on this day?' He said that he did.

'Well,' I said, 'If I were foolish enough to do what you want today do you know what would happen?'

He asked what would happen.

I said that neither men nor steamer nor cargo would ever be seen anymore. 'Don't you know that island is a dead leeshore today?'

The Commander said, 'What do you mean by a dead leeshore?'

And I said 'Maister, sometimes I have thought you did not understand much pertaining to a seaman's life. But now you have confirmed my doubts.'

And I tried to explain to him what is meant by a dead leeshore. Yet he had charge of most of all the merchant vessels which came to Scapa Flow, and there he was not able to understand what is meant by a dead leeshore.

Needless to say we had a few narrow escapes while we were attached to our Grand Fleet. We found the men on board the American battleships very obliging though. While we were passing one of these ships at anchor in Scapa Flow – *Wyoming* was her name – we asked the officer on the watch if we could lay alongside while we had our dinner. The officer thought we had asked if we could have our dinner onboard his ship and called to us to hold on for a few minutes. Then he disappeared but returned in a great hurry saying that it was all right for us to come onboard and to bring all the crew and have dinner with them.

We thanked him kindly but explained that our dinner was ready and we only wanted to lay alongside during dinner hour. Some of the American crew came on board our steamer and when they heard that I had stayed in the U.S.A. for seven years and nine months they became very friendly, and thereafter always hailed us when we passed by.

While I was home on leave one time our steamer was ordered to go alongside a certain few of our battle fleet, and then alongside an old battle ship, the *Royal Arthur*, which was anchored just inside the defence booms in Hoxa Sound in Scapa Flow. Between the *Royal Arthur* and the Grand Fleet there were three rows of mines. We had been alongside the *Royal Arthur* several times and our mate who was in charge in my absence and who received the orders, wanted to go through the passage we had always gone. But the officer in charge would not allow our mate to go that way and he was forced to obey wrong orders.

When nearing the *Royal Arthur* the crew of the *Maggie Lough* saw a crowd collected on the ship's fokselhead. The commander called by megaphone, '*Maggie Lough* ahoy, are you coming alongside?' Our mate answered that they were. The Commander asked then who had given orders for them to come the way that they did and when our mate told him, the Commander danced with rage.

A few minutes later he said to our mate, 'You have revealed something to us this morning. We never thought any boat could come near us in the way you have come. Everyone onboard this ship had been expecting to see you blown to atoms. Do you know that you have come over three rows of mines which we thought impregnable? The wonder is, how did you escape disaster. But the officer who gave you such orders will hear about this today.'

We were kept very busy night and day and often riding with two anchors on dark winter nights with not even a light in our cabin while at mealtimes on account of Zeppelins. Life was not pleasant at these times, for very often when we were at anchor and expected we were finished and had set the watch, orders came through that we had to go out to meet another steamer from Shetland. Our crew were very tired after battling all day with wind and sea – but we always had to obey our orders, and we never really knew when we were finished. Many days we had no food to eat at all.

One Christmas week we returned to our parent ship on a wild and wintry night. The crew were very tired and hungry, but the canteen officer had just finished and he refused us food. So we had to find a safe anchorage for the night. But it kept snowing and blowing a great storm for some days. One little steamer had loaded a cargo of Christmas presents for the Grand Fleet but the weather was too bad for them to get near the Grand Fleet. The master of the little steamer had been ordered to distribute the presents amongst the smaller craft sheltering under the lee of the islands and we got a glad surprise when the steamer came alongside and we were told we could have some Christmas presents.

We could hardly believe it was true until we received a crate filled with pheasants, partridges and such like. Also a large box of plum puddings and I am sure that Mrs McPherson and many other ladies' ears would ring, for our crew did bless each one of these ladies that afternoon. We had plum puddings and pheasants that night and next morning and a few days afterwards.

And when the storm moderated we went alongside an English boat, which had just arrived the day before the storm came on. The crew were actually starving. I said to these poor men, 'A merry Christmas to you boys!'

They replied 'A hungry Christmas you should say.'

I said, 'Would you accept a plum pudding?' and they turned away from me in disgust. They were starving and could not believe their own eyes when I handed them three plum puddings. They said, 'Are these really for us?' Their eyes sparkled with gladness and their mouths watered. A plum pudding is a sweet morsel to an Englishman, but more so that day as their stomachs were empty.

We had learned to do without sugar in our tea sometime previous, and the war had taught us to do without many luxuries and even bare necessities were very sweet. We had managed all right up to that date. We had a few narrow escapes, though these were got through. But one day I found three telegrams waiting for me when I came in from the sea.

One telegram read 'Mother very sick. Will wire you later'.

The next one read 'Mother serious, you better come home'.

The third one read 'Come home at once, mother much worse'.

And from that time on our troubles increased.

Both the mail-boat and the train seemed to creep along and I had to wait seven hours at Edinburgh, which seemed like a week. But at last I arrived and saw very plainly my partner-in-life was nearing the shore. And I soon would miss her wise counsel. However I stood by her night and day for five weeks. The Admiralty kindly allowed our boys to see their mother before she died. But they had to join their boat and their parting with their mother cannot be told neither by word nor pen.

And it has been made very plain to me that when Mother passed away our defence was broken and ill or ills have befallen our home ever since. We have been unable to ward them off.

While I was at home the *SS Maggie Lough* was ordered to load a cargo of building materials to erect a listening station at Fair Isle. At that time these parts were infested with German submarines and mines. The cargo had to be ferried on to the island and put so-many-feet above high water mark, and for that purpose a large rowing boat was put on our steamer's deck. But a storm came on while on the voyage. Heavy seas broke over the steamer and there were great dangers of the large row boat smashing a hole in the engine room casing which would have been serious. To save us from that calamity our steamer had to be put head out to sea, and that caused her to get amongst the mines. We had to choose between being blown to pieces by the mines or swamped by the heavy seas. And only by good seamanship did we reach Fair Isle.

The crew had to ferry cargo onshore and whenever it was finished they were ordered off to sea. Our crew had never rested but had to obey orders, even though the weather was still very bad and the sea very heavy.

When we were a few miles out, and while the engineer was repairing the pumps orders came to proceed to return to Fair Isle again – and they went, even though the weather was still very bad.

Signals were sent to them again to return once more, but this time they refused and after many long and weary hours battling with the wind and the sea, the steamer arrived at Scapa Flow. The crew were exhausted, the boat half full of water, yet orders were received to load at once another cargo for Fair Isle. But the crew were unable to stand on their feet and each man fell asleep where they were.

A few hours later our engineer, my son Robert, awoke suffering terribly. He developed double pneumonia. The crew put him on board the mail boat on Monday and I received a letter on the Thursday from my second son who was in charge of our *SS Maggie Lough* saying that he hoped his brother Robert had arrived home safely. That was the first we had heard about our engineer being sick and we wondered where he could be or what had happened to him. And I began in real earnest to search for him, and I found him in Perth Infirmary at eight o'clock on Saturday night, almost a week after he had left. He had lost consciousness after changing trains at Perth railway station and had lain outside all night until some Good Samaritan kindly conveyed him to the Infirmary. His kit bag went on to Cardiff in Wales and was only recovered after many weeks of waiting.

Many weeks afterwards Robert was sent home from hospital, but he never really recovered. He went to sea for nearly two years after, but the voyage to Fair Isle had left its mark on one of the best and strongest men. He withered away. When he left *SS Maggie Lough* at Scapa Flow he said to our second engineer, 'Now John. Don't allow any strange engineer to do anything to our engine.'

John, our youngest boy was only seventeen years old, and had been on the service no more than one year. So John promised Robert that no man would get the chance to repair our engine until Robert came back to our steamer – and John tried his very best to keep the engine and the boiler in first class order.

I had joined the *SS Maggie Lough* again when Robert turned sick and remained until April 4th 1919 when we were discharged. I put the *SS Maggie Lough* into drydock and the Admiralty gave me five-hundred-and-twenty pounds to pay for the reconditioning of our steamer. But the first account I received was twelve-hundred pounds, and the final total was near fifteen-hundred pounds. I had spent four hundred pounds of my money during the service for repairs to the steamer. This made the account for repairs for the past years service during the war nineteen-hundred pounds, yet the Admiralty only made me a final offer of five-hundred-and-twenty pounds and I would have had to go to court to try to get more.

After the repairs were finished we started running cargoes of coal to Aberdeen and Peterhead and soon we were running three cargoes per week. These two steamers of ours ran more cargoes than any other two steamers on our coast for the same length of time.

My youngest son John kept the engine and boiler in fine condition. Though the hard war service had ruined his health also, yet he kept going for two years after the war. Then he could not work anymore and withered away like the flower after spring and died 1923, February 18th.

On the day that he was compelled to leave our *SS Maggie Lough* John begged Jamie not to engage an engineer, only a fireman, and that he would soon came back to steam again. And though Jamie had plenty of work to do on deck, yet he promised to oil and look after the engine.

But one year later, after we had done repairs and made ready for the winter, I received a telephone call from the local doctor telling me that he had spoken to Jamie. He said that if I wanted to save Jamie I had better stop him going to sea any more. I had cleaned the boiler and had steam

ready to sail the next morning, so that news from the doctor gave me a
shock, but I made up my mind to sell the *SS Maggie Lough*.

At once I cancelled the cargo and wrote some letters to folk whom I
was acquainted with and next day there were two buyers who were after
our steamer.

Steaming Days, Happy as Seabirds

In this chapter James returns to the time before the Great War when he was building up his coastal business. As well as relying on his elder son, he reveals the importance to the family unit of his wife and of his three daughters, Agnes, Jean and Jamesena. Let down by the dock labourers of Leith, James's girls rolled up their sleeves and helped store barrels of herring which the crew were unloading from the SS Maggie Lough.

Perhaps had it not been for the outbreak of the war, then Lough would have added a fleet to the two little ships he owned. Perhaps he might have been as much of an entrepreneur on the Scottish coast as John Craig was on the North American Great Lakes.

One company had been our rivals for several years and had tried their very best to swamp me, and even threatened to take the work at Eyemouth from me, but failed. And after they had done their best to do me, they were honest enough to tell me the incident which made them give up trying any more.

We were very busy running cargoes of cured herring to continental steamers at Leith and my three daughters had come with us onboard our *SS Maggie Lough*. We were busy discharging on Saturday and half our cargo was out when the whistle blew at noon. The dock labourers promised to come back after dinner to finish discharging but did not return.

Our rivals, whose office was near the dock, saw our plight and were very pleased. But a while later our three girls – Agnes, Jean and Jamesena – came down from Edinburgh. They had their good clothes on, but when they saw us idle and learned the cause they consulted each other. I had advised them to go home by train, but they asked if our crew would land the herring in barrels on to the dockside. We said yes, and they stripped off their good clothes and found enough wrapping which they fastened around themselves and they rolled every barrel into the shed.

We sailed for home that same evening and our rivals were watching us from their office window. These men told us the next day when we were at Leith they would never try to beat me again. They were convinced after they saw our three girls take off their good clothes and roll all these barrels of herring that they would lose their money if they persisted in trying to get the better of us.

Several shipbrokers offered to take shares in a new steamer with me - and more than one ship builder offered to build and furnish it with an engine and a whole outfit and then give me time to work them clear. But I preferred to work my own steamer.

Though it meant a very busy life and very little sleep, yet I found great interest in the work and I gained much knowledge which I never would have learned if I had been sailing under owners. For I made the acquaintance of very many merchants in most of the shipping ports around our coast.

I benefited more in Great Yarmouth than any other port, seeing loading berths are so scarce at that port. Many Captains of steamers often wondered how I managed to get loaded and away to sea before they could get a start to load. The conditions were that when I had got a cargo of herring to load then whenever the last barrel came on board and ropes were cast off, we just had to go to sea. And that happened more than once. Except when in port on a Sunday morning I could not sleep more than one hour and a half at a time.

I often had a good laugh at myself after I had got my cargo made up. I used to get amongst the Russian Jews who were to be found in large numbers in the fish market at Yarmouth. These men soon learned to know me and each of them booked so-many-barrels of cured herring for Russian ports. I could deal much better with these men than any broker could do. It was seldom that I ever needed a ship broker.

I found enough cargoes to keep both steamers busy and sometimes I had to engage another two steamers to help us. Of course we worked very hard and saved money quickly and could have had a fleet of coasting steamers busy along our coast. The dock masters at Aberdeen, Burntisland and Grangemouth and other ports treated us kindly, but especially at Aberdeen. Many times the dockmaster there held the gates open to let us get out even when we were more than twenty minutes late. The dock men and bridge men were all friendly towards us and were anxious that we should break all records. Three cargoes per week were the most any steamer had run. We ran four cargoes from Saturday to Saturday, but were just a few minutes late to get into the dock – though if we had sounded our whistle a few minutes earlier we would have got into dock.

I put my brother as master of our steamer the *SS Maggie Purves* and he had engaged a crew of his own men and loaded a cargo of coal for Arbroath. But they were caught in a storm and these men, not being acquainted with heavy laded crafts, got a little scared and put in here at Eyemouth windbound with a cargo of ore near to Christmas day. The crew wanted to stay in port until after the New Year. My brother the Captain had lumbago in his back and could not go out with the steamer.

I was much afraid of the cargo staying too long in the steamer's hold, and so I went myself in charge of the *SS Maggie Purves* and arrived at Wellington Quay, River Tyne at midnight on a Saturday and moored alongside a coal hulk.

The crew had a rest all Sunday, and at nine-thirty all hands turned in for the night. Our mate on that trip was a big, heavy weight who lay in the lower after bed. The deckhand in the upper bed very soon began to howl like those who have nightmares. Our mate rose out of his bed intending to rouse our deckhand out of the nightmare, but to my astonishment our mate fell on the cabin floor as if dead, and the deckhand still kept howling in a strange manner. I tried to lift our mate up the companion steps, but then I lost consciousness and both of us fell to the cabin floor. I had struck my head against the cabin stove and I lost a lot of blood.

I lay unconscious quite a while before being discovered by our engineer who had joined the steamer just before leaving Eyemouth. He went for the watchman onboard the coal hulk. These two men saw us lying unconscious but had not the courage to come and help us. Instead they telephoned the river police to say that three of the steamer *SS Maggie Purves'* crew were dead.

Our steamer was moored with her head down the river and her stern to the wind which was blowing strong, and because I was lying at the foot of the companion stairs the wind brought me round and I recovered my senses. My mate and deckhand were still lying unconscious, and I felt very weak through loss of blood yet my heart yearned to save these two men and I resolved to make another desperate effort and managed to get the deckhand up to the top of the companion stairs. The cool night wind revived him also. Meanwhile I struggled with our mate who, as I stated, was a heavy man and had a large family to provide for. I managed to get him in front of me seated on my knees and up, one step at a time. The wind blew on to his face which brought him to his senses once more.

All three of us were sitting on deck, enjoying the cool night breeze after our sickness and we discussed the cause of our strange experience and found it was the fumes from our cargo which was almost proved fatal to all three of us. At that moment a boat came near and hailed us.

'Steamer ahoy' he said.

I said, 'Hullo.'

'What steamer are you?'

'Maggie Purves' I replied.

'Alright' he said, 'here are the stretchers.'

'What?' I said.

'The stretchers for the three dead men of your crew.'

I said that he was mistaken and that all of our crew were alive. 'We are the river police and have brought a doctor and also three stretchers which you telephoned for,' the man shouted.

I informed him that I had never phoned and we found that it was our engineer who was still with the night watchman on board the coal hulk and who might have saved all that trouble if he had played his part like a man ought to do. The river police handed me a bill a few weeks later for their one-hour's outing. For my part I never got as much as a thank you for the loss of all that fine scotch blood and for risking my own life. Yet I had done what I considered to be my duty and saved these two lives. The River Police bill amounted to three-pounds-fifteen shillings, which I paid.

On the Monday morning we moored at Wellington Quay and I saw the manager of the works who informed me they were so busy that we could not get discharged for another eight days. Of course after the previous night's experience I was very much afraid of the fumes doing any more harm, and I was determined to leave no stone unturned in order to have the cargo discharged. So I went up to Hepburn and moored alongside a large steamer which was being unloaded and I hunted the manager. There I gained my point and started discharging.

The next morning the captain came at me like a wild man. They had been waiting to discharge several sailing ships for many days and were angry with me. But I told them plain that they must keep up with the times and get a steamer. Neither had I got one but two steamers by that time – and yet it was hard work to make ends meet.

That voyage seemed to be full of mishaps, for I lost my watch overboard that night. We loaded salt at Middlesboro next day and my crew being all strange to our boat I was at the wheel from the time we left the salt wharf until we were north of the Tyne.

Many times the weather was very foggy with frost rind, while at other times it was clear and our mate, who was a good seaman, was very anxious to relieve me at the wheel. He was very much hurt when I refused to let him. I tried to explain to him in a kindly way my reason for refusing him while the fog lasted, but he argued that he knew the boat as well as most men. I was aware he knew the boat, but he didn't know the tricks our small steamer played with strangers during foggy weather.

'But,' said he, 'there is Tynemouth pier lights, and also St Marys and Blyth lights.'

'Yes,' I said, 'but it may be very dense in a short time.'

'Well' he said, 'I will call on you if it becomes dense. Coffee is ready. You had better have some.'

I said, 'You call me immediately the fog comes on.'

There was a long ground-swell from the north east, but the wind blew West-North-West. I had some warm coffee which was very fine after my long stand at the wheel on a cold winter's night. I sat near a warm fire and I was loath to leave it, but while I was enjoying a few minutes after supper I felt the steamer touch against something hard. She ran near her own length on top of the rocks.

It was two hours after high water then, which enabled me to keep very cool. But our mate – poor soul – was in a terrible way and could not forgive himself. I had warned him to call me whenever the fog came, but he was anxious that I should have a little rest. I had given him the course to steer and warned him that every sheer would be to port, which in a little while might be serious unless he was careful to bring the steamer to starboard as much as she had gone to port. That was my reason for being so much afraid to let our mate or anyone else take the wheel on our voyage north until they were better acquainted with our steamer. Had the weather kept clear all would have been well. However, at the time we ran aground, the fog was dense.

Yet I had a good idea where we were, and unless the wind changed the steamer would not get into too much harm. We ran out the anchor astern as a precaution and I tried my best to cheer our mate who was very unhappy. To make matters worse the wind shifted around to the south east, and then we were on a leeshore when the flood tide came on. This made us feel uncomfortable, but we managed to get clear of the rocks undamaged.

All then went well until we came near Eyemouth. The night was very dark and I could tell by the high north-east swell that the sea would be breaking heavy at the harbour entrance, and I cautioned our engineer to have enough steam handy for any emergency. But when we were between the rocks, a high sea broke over our boat. Our engineer had let the steam down to low. When a big sea threatened to run our boat on to the beach I ordered the engine to be slowed down, but the engineer stopped the engine completely and with the steam being very low he could not start it up again. It was so much needed to cross the harbour bar, and we were then at the mercy of the breakers with a strong current coming against us out of the harbour. At the very moment when all seemed lost, the throttle of the engine opened full out and the engine started just as a heavy sea struck the steamer. She was fairly heading for the entrance to the harbour and each man said 'Thank God' as the steamer ran between the piers, safe for another time.

So that had been a very exciting voyage, but only one amongst many which we dared not think too much about. They all help to make up a sailor's life and whenever cargo was discharged we were out on the briny again, happy as the seabirds.

Our insurance limits were Lerwick to London, Brest and Hamburg and all round the British Isles. If we wanted to go beyond these limits we had to pay extra insurance, but I always found enough cargoes to keep both steamers busy and never needed to go beyond our insurance limits.

Remembering the Past, Happy with the Present

*Here Lough returns to documenting his early months in America and the
arrival of his wife and children – an arrival that was delayed because of an
illness which struck baby Jamesena, who had been born after James had left
Scotland.*

*He also recalls some of the harsh scrapes that befell him, both in Ohio and
at home in Britain and ends the chapter with a story about how at the age of
seventy-one he dived into the harbour at Eyemouth to rescue a small boy who
had fallen in. Though he does not say so, he handed his jacket to his
companion who had been walking down the quay with him: it was his
fourteen-year-old granddaughter Peggy Dale. When Lough's memoirs surfaced after eighty years she listened intently and then exclaimed at this point:
'I was there. That was me he handed his jacket to!'*

After I had been nine months in the U.S.A. my wife and children went to
Glasgow. Maggie's aunt Jean went with them to see them sail on the
following day. They stayed in a friend's house overnight, and the next
day my wife's aunt saw them on board the steamer *Prussian*. But the
sailors went on strike and the steamer was delayed for three days. During
that time our youngest child Jamesena, who was only three months old,
contracted chicken pox. However Aunt Jeanie saw my wife and children
sail away down the Clyde and then went back to stay at her friend's
house till the following morning.

The *SS Prussian* was anchored at the tail of the bank, and a doctor
came on board to inspect the passengers and found two or three chicken
pox on our Jamesena and ordered mother and children ashore. They
were landed at Greenock. It was near dark and my wife had never been in
that part of the country, and felt very downcast. All her luggage went
with the *SS Prussian,* and where was she to go with her four children that
night? But she braced herself up, found a train to Glasgow and located
the house where Aunt Jeanie had stayed.

But only a little girl was at home. Aunt Jeanie and her friend had gone out to view Glasgow. So a surprise awaited them when they entered the house. My wife and children had to go home for three months after this. I meantime (in the U.S.A.) watched for the arrival of the *SS Prussian* and went to Detroit to meet the boat train from Windsor. I waited until every passenger had passed out of the depot, wondering what had happened to those I counted more dear to me than life. But after a while a telegram arrived and explained matters and I went back to my work.

After three months I learned that my wife and bairns had sailed for Montreal aboard the *SS Norwegian*. The present Mr Craig's father – old Uncle George our children always used to call him – was so very anxious to meet my wife and children, and his home being in Detroit, he sent me strict orders not to leave my work. He would attend to them and said that after a few hours he would see them onboard the passenger steamer for Toledo. I told him to arrange with the Captain to land my wife and family at the wheeling bridge about one mile and a half below Craig Shipyard. My acquaintance had a nice supper ready for my wife and family for when they would arrive.

But my brother-in-law Willie Purves who had been at Detroit came with my folks and he omitted to inform the Captain of my request. They did not stop at the bridge. I then went up river in a row boat after the steamer and I saw our children pass on to the landing station. I saw a few men who were wrangling about who would pay for carting all the luggage to Craig's shipyard, and I explained in a few seconds that I would. I then hurried on to the street, expecting to overtake my family in a few minutes. I hurried along Summit Street, across the bridge but I could not locate them. I turned and re-crossed the bridge, and then called at all the hotels in the city. But still I could not find any trace of them. So I informed the police and then went home – but no better luck there either. I was tired out but I could not rest and I returned to the city and I searched everywhere, before finally returning again to the shipyard – and there found my family at the door of our home!

At once I forgot about all my anxious hours. We were very happy in each other's company. My brother-in-law had taken my family into a street car which runs down the opposite side of the river from the shipyard, and a kind lady noticed their plight and invited them into her house where they stayed all evening. So we will not forget their first night in Toledo.

Some weeks later I brought a boatload of light lumber, which was much longer than the rowboat. One end went under the foremost seat and the other out over the stern, which I well fastened securely. The river is about one mile broad, and when I was about in the middle of the river a severe thunderstorm burst with great fury. The wind gusted under the lumber and lifted the boat's stern out of the water. The next moment I was underneath the boat, but I managed to get out from there and climbed on to the upturned bottom. But the next moment the boat turned over and I was underneath again. I managed on board once more, but she played me the same trick. I was feeling very tired and decided to hold on to the keel near the bow until the boat drove towards the shore.

There were lots of boats at the shipyard but no one dared to come to help me. The wind blew so strong that I could hear Mr Craig calling to me to hold on. I tried to signal him that all was well and managed to scurry to the shore.

A few weeks later I brought six young men off a sailing yacht which capsized a little way from the shipyard, but a sad end happened to their six young women companions who were all drowned in the cabin when the yacht capsized. The six young men who were on deck never had the presence of mind to break the side of the cabin and save the young ladies. The yacht drove onshore, but all were drowned, four sisters among them. Thunderstorms were very severe in that part of the world.

Sometime later I had a strange experience while working in the Malleable Iron Works. I had got my hand a little hurt and the Superintendent gave me what he thought was an easier job. But while at this work a high wall fell over and, along with a lot of others, I was buried with debris which covered me up to my under lip.

I had a few other narrow escapes. One time when I was master of the *SS Maggie Purves* we were discharging potatoes in bulk at Newcastle quay. I had ordered the dry dock to be ready for three o'clock in the afternoon and I was anxious to be ready for it opening. We had twenty tons in the fore part of the hold, against four in the bulkhead and I tried to hurry the work. At that moment a steamer passed by and the swell from his paddles caused our boat to plunge a little. The potatoes fell on top of me and I was very badly hurt, and nearly despaired of ever going to sea again.

But after a few months I went back to the sea. It was long before I should have gone, but I was in debt and anxious to pay it off.

A few years later when I was master of the steamer the *SS Maggie*

Lough we arrived at Stockton-on-Tees with a cargo of ore. We worked all night discharging the cargo and then came down the river to Tennants Wharf, Middlesbrough and started loading salt into bags at eight am. At eight thirty my mate and I were seeing to the loading, with the crane lowering sixteen bags in each sling. The men on the dock were hurrying to finish in time for the football match, so perhaps they were not careful enough. One bag slipped out of the sling and dropped over thirty feet 'end on'. It struck me between my shoulders a sliding blow which knocked me down the steamer's hold. That hurt me very badly, but the fall into the hold saved my life – for the next moment the other fifteen bags of salt dropped out of the sling and fell onto the deck at the very spot where I was standing. They would certainly have crushed me to death.

That accident happened at eight thirty Saturday morning. It was two thirty pm when I arrived at Middlesbrough Infirmary. I should have been well compensated for my injuries, but I was anxious to get on board the steamer again and settled without giving any trouble.

I omitted to state that while working in the Malleable Iron Works in Toledo, U.S.A. I had been painting the tall chimneys and sometimes I reported that the bricks which the chimneys were lined up with inside had expanded so much that they had burst all of the rivet heads off. It was only the bricks which were holding the tall chimneys up.

The managers felt somewhat anxious regarding the matter and consulted their bricklayer, who proposed to cut sections of the bricks out, re-rivet the chimney and then build the sections up with new bricks. All went well for two days until the bricklayer was working thirty feet up. I had fitted a piece of wood across the top of the chimney so that it could not shift. I also fastened a block with tackle and that way did hoist the bricklayer up to work – who was a Scotchman, John McFadden by name.

Mr Booth, the Superintendent, came to see how the work was proceeding and asked my opinion on the job. We were standing right under the bricklayer and he heard me tell Mr Booth that I felt very uncomfortable and I was certain that there would be an accident before the bricklayer got much higher. A large crowd of moulders were working nearby and Mr Booth gave all of these men orders to shift to the other building that very evening, and this was the means of saving their lives.

The bricklayer and I started work as usual the next morning, and at about eleven o'clock I informed the bricklayer that I felt alarmed about the work that he was doing. I noticed while I was hoisting the bricks and fire-clay up the chimney to him that they did not keep the centre, but scraped against the side. I was sure the tall chimney was beginning to lean over to one side. But the bricklayer would not believe it and argued that the piece of wood which I had fixed across the top of the chimney had shifted.

I knew that was impossible. But to satisfy him I offered to go to the top and make certain. But he said it was near time for dinner. 'You can go up after dinner'.

In a short time he said, 'Lower me down for a few minutes.' Which I did.

I have many times since thought he was feeling nervous over the work. However he said, 'I must go up again. It is rather early for dinner'.

He was actually into the boatswain's chair and I was ready to hoist him up when a loud report warned us we must run for our lives . . . He along one side of the melting furnace and I along the other side and we jumped from the front of the furnace to the ground. The tall chimney had fallen and smashed the wall and the roof and eighty feet long beams.

I fell when I jumped from the top of the furnace and in my hurry I ran on hands and feet. The roof slates and the great beams falling all around made the place dark with falling debris. But I saw a glimmer of light which I headed for. I thought it would be the door on the opposite side of the building. I found I was right, and after a breath of fresh air I wondered what had happened to McFadden. I called to him but no answer came. I went to search for him and found him in front of the furnace. He had fainted as he leapt from the top, and I had quite a job to get him over the debris and out into the fresh air. I thought he had been hit by the falling beams or stones and was afraid he was dead, but after a while he showed signs of life.

At that time all those men employed in the works were searching for us amongst the wreckage and were very pleased to see us alive. Had Mr Booth delayed sending these moulders to another shop, the loss of life would have been very great.

McFadden did not come to work for a few days. He had got a shock to his nerves, and I have often wondered what would have happened to my nerves if I had gone to inspect the wood on the top of the chimney as I had offered to do.

The question is often asked, '*Can any good come out of evil?*'
Well, the falling of that chimney raised me very considerably in my
employers' estimation and they counted the hours I had worked on those
chimneys and paid me extra for each hour, which amounted to a nice
little sum.

And I learned that my employers always sent to Chicago for a man to
splice their rope belts used in the machinery. When they heard that I
could do that work they paid me well instead of sending to Chicago for a
man, and in other ways did they try to encourage me.

I omitted to mention the first winter we were in Trenton, U.S.A. we
looked after four large steamers. We had dinner in the boarding house of
Mrs Lafrance, but slept on board one of the steamers where we made our
breakfast and tea (or supper as it is called in the U.S.A.). We lifted a few
hatches off on fine mornings and put them on again each night. We saw
that the moorings were secure and we were paid one dollar per day for
that work.

A man and his wife looked after four steamers on the opposite side of
the river. Mr Bingham worked beside us in Craig's Shipyard and we were
very friendly – Mrs Bingham made warm scones for our tea each day.
After our day's work was finished we crossed the river on the ice for our
warm scones, which were very nice, and we enjoyed our evening meal
together.

As we left the steamer one morning in early spring 1890 I called my
brother-in-law's attention to the condition of the ice, which did not look
safe. But Willie thought I was getting nervous and paid no heed to my
warning. So, after the day's work finished in the shipyard we crossed the
river as usual. Mrs Bingham lowered our warm scones over the steamer's
side to us and we hurried up river to our boat named the *Gettysburg*.
While we were passing the steamer *Volunteer's* bow I cautioned my
brother-in-law regarding the ice being unsafe. He was twenty paces
ahead of me, and thirty feet from our flat bottomed skiff which was
moored at the rear of the steamer *Gettysburg*.

Willie went through the ice. He could not swim one stoke and the
water was deep and there was a real danger of him getting under the ice. I
tried to reach him but the ice gave way under me too and now there were
two of us in that hole. Willie struggled hard and I had to be careful he did
not get hold of me. No one was near to help, as all the workmen had
gone home by then. We made quite a large hole in the ice. I got behind

Willie, pushing him up stream and breaking the ice as we went. I was very tired when we got hold of the flat-bottomed boat.

After we were in the boat I lifted my hat and we saw all our nice scones floating in the water. I said, 'What will be have for tea Willie? Look at our scones!'

And I plunged in and collected the dainties. I then climbed on board the *Gettysburg* and we lighted the stove and had our tea ready as soon as possible. Our appetite was very keen that evening after our hard day's work and overtime.

But the immersion had not agreed with Willie. He turned ill during the night and did not work for two months and I thought he was going to die.

Mr and Mrs Craig took him to their home for several weeks and nursed him, which brought him back to normal health again.

A few months before sailing to the U.S.A. we had just arrived home in Eyemouth from Great Yarmouth. I had washed and had shifted my clothing and was on my way down to the harbour when I heard someone calling that a boy had fallen in. I saw lots of folks running and sure enough the boy had sunk beneath the surface. He was only a few yards from the pier – it might have been our boy, I didn't know who it was. I jumped into the harbour and got the boy out who was nearly drowned. The father and mother were very thankful for the boy being restored to them.

I have been the means of saving another four lives at great risk to my own life. It cost me five-pounds-fifteen-shillings for repairing my watch after struggling in the water to save an eight year old boy whose home was in Edinburgh. I was seventy-one years old then and I swallowed some filthy water which poisoned my stomach and caused me much trouble. Yet after my hard sea faring life and all the ills which have befallen me, I try to smile to all that I meet. The days are too short, I cannot find the time to do all that I want to do and I never lose or waste one Golden Hour.

I did not get much time at school when a boy. I only remember having two books and I had to look on some other boy's book. Yet I was anxious to get an education. I was the oldest of seven children and had to gather mussels and limpets to bait my father's lines, and on that account I had to stay away from the school. But after I had been at the fishing a few years I bought books on navigation and learned what I could.

I always hankered after the merchant service, and even while in the U.S.A. I always thought if I could get a start in that line I would do well.

After the great Disaster here in 1881 my brothers-in-law failed to find a man who would take their father's place aboard their father's fishing boat, he having been lost in that terrible storm when one hundred and twenty nine brave men found a watery grave. His name was James Purves and he drowned on board the *Myrtle*.

John Purves was a few years my senior yet he had not confidence in himself to manage a fishing boat. After much persuasion I consented to find a good fisherman to go in my place in our boat along with my father and my brother who was nineteen years old. He was anxious to push ahead.

So I shipped onboard the *Border Rose* and two months later my brother Robert, whom my hope for the future was built on, was knocked overboard and drowned. I have never forgiven myself and never will my foolish act in leaving our own family boat.

But I have had many more hard knocks since then and I am now near seventy-two years and six months old and thinking on having another long sea voyage. I have lots of friends and acquaintances in many different sea ports.

God has blessed me with a cheerful heart which is better than great riches.

Back in America

James Lough lived out the dotage of his years at number seventeen George Street, Eyemouth where he was cared for by his extended family, the Loughs and the Windrams. To make room for everyone, an additional level was added to the property.

James enjoyed sitting at the quayside, walking along the harbour and taking the occasional sea voyage up or down the coast. He spoke often and at length of his time in America and returned twice to the country that he would have loved to have been his home. The first time, in 1922, he ventured only to Toledo. Six years later James criss-crossed from east to west where he visited Scottish people in several states as well as in Canada. He then made his way south to California where he spent time with John Craig's sons and their families who had founded the new yard at Long Beach. He then returned across the central United States, snaking his way back to Toledo, where he stayed with his brother-in-law Willie Purves and enjoyed the company of his old friends, Mr and Mrs Craig. While in Ohio James obtained citizenship papers for his son Jamie who had been born in Toledo in 1893. Like his father, the young lad was keen to grasp the American dream. Like his father, Jamie intended finding work with his cousins the Craigs – and was all set to move to California.

But young Jamie Lough never made it to Long Beach. Along with his brothers John and Robert, Jamie had suffered ill health from the time of his service in the merchant marine during the Great War. He wasted away and died in 1929 just a year after his father had secured his American citizenship and a matter of weeks after James Lough completed this memoir.

After twenty-seven years I returned to visit my friends in the U.S.A. and found Mrs Craig lamenting the loss of her daughter Katie. Mrs Craig was very distressed. I tried to say something to console her but words seem very empty when our hearts are bleeding. Time helps to soothe, yet the wound never really heals up. I had lost my dear wife a short while previous who always thought Mrs Craig was her very dear friend and on that account Mrs Craig allowed me to say to her what was in my heart, and in that way my own wound had balm poured on it.

I visited my brother-in-law Willie Purves and stayed with his family for sometime. They treated me very kindly. I went to Craig's shipyard and didn't know the place; the changes had been great. It was only when the street car stopped at the foot of York Street that I saw my own house which had been my home for seven exciting years. Then I understood that I had passed the Malleable Iron Works and the shipyard where I had worked for those seven years.

I went to the office at the Shipyard's main entrance and there the day watchman rose from his seat and said to me 'Where do you wish be sir?'

I replied, 'I want into the shipyard.'

'Where is your pass?' said he.

'A pass?' said I. 'I never thought on asking for a pass'.

'Well,' said the watchman, 'You don't get any further that way without a pass'.

'Well my man,' I said, 'You will not get into any trouble through me. But I will be in this shipyard today. Kindly tell me the manager's name.'

He said his name was Henderson. 'Then he is a Scotchman'.

'You are right, and he is in. Will you allow me to knock on the door of his office? Do you know him?' said the watchman.

I said that I did not know him, but added 'Surely you will let me knock on his office door?' I did not wait for his answer, but pushed ahead and chapped at the door. Someone called 'Come in' and in I went.

'Are you Mr Henderson?'

'Yes,' he said, 'What can I do for you?'

I said 'You can let me through into the shipyard if you please. I want to have another look at the old place.'

And he looked hard at me and said, 'The old place? That suggests to me that you have been here before. How long ago was that?'

I replied 'Before the Craigs came to work here.'

Then his face took on a queer smile because he thought he had me in a fix. He grinned and then said that they had been the first here. I knew what was in his mind. But I was no impostor. 'I worked here six months before the Craigs left Trenton. I was the first workman in this yard.' At that Henderson said 'You will get through. Go where you wish, stay as long as you want to, but don't go away without seeing me. Come here before you leave. Here is a pass for you.'

And I had a great day out. I went down to the dock which I had helped to build and oh! How quickly my memory travelled. I had done all the sheet spilling round all the docks, and many other jobs which I remembered that day. I then wandered amongst the workmen. I spoke to one who was stooping down marking off a piece of timber.

'Can you tell me where Bill Carter is working?' I said.

He straightened himself up as he spoke and I recognised him at once and said 'Hullo Tommy Bowden! How are you getting on?'

And with a surprised look he said, 'I don't know who you are?'

'But you *are* Tommy Bowden' I said.

'Yes'

'Well,' I said, 'This is me!'

'Yes, well that is you, but who are you?' And with that Tommy looked around to see if the foreman was near. I said, 'You are alright Tommy. I have the freedom of the yard today.' But still he wondered who I was. Then I reminded him of the man who engaged him to carry water to the workmen in the shipyard and with that he grasped my hand very tight and asked lots of questions. He told me where to find Bill Carter and many more of my old work-mates who gave me a very warm welcome.

I found Mr Henderson the manager, and also the Superintendent waiting for me in the office. They sent for many of the men who I had not seen whilst in the yard that day. These two men did enjoy the surprise each got when they come into the office. Mr Henderson introduced me to each one as their old friend and work-mate and not one knew me. Mr Henderson and the Superintendent did enjoy the surprised look and antics of each man when I told them who I was.

We were all astonished when the whistle blew at the close of the day's work. It was a proof that there are no friends like old friends.

Next day I went to the Malleable Iron Works and I could not help going to see the tall chimneys and perhaps I said something to each of them. You see I had done a lot for them. One time a workman went to the top of one chimney and turned dizzy and dared not move. I had quite a risky job to take him to earth. I met him that day and we laughed together regarding the incident, though it happened twenty-seven years previous.

Meeting so many of these old friends made my holiday a real joy.

Few men, if any, ever had so many friends amongst the work-mates who received a welcome such as I got. And after six years I again had a hankering to see my old and tried friends Mr and Mrs Craig and my brother-in-law William Purves and family and I was fully rewarded for the journey for I was well treated in both of these homes – and after two months stay I bought a stop off ticket for California.

I left Toledo on 2nd June 1928 and stopped a few days with friends in Chicago. Next stop was Sovereign Saskatchewan, Canada with my friend Rev Alex and Mrs Robertson where I stayed seven days. Next stop was Edmonton for another seven days. I had no address but had very little difficulty in finding these folks home. And our hearts were sore when we parted.

I stayed a few days with Eyemouth folks at New Westminster and seven days at Vancouver with Mr and Mrs Reid who were extremely kind. I saw several more families at Vancouver who were my relations – and also a Captain who was master for sometime of the famous clipper Cutty Sark. I told him that I came from the same little town as the owner of the famous ship – John 'Jock' Whillis was an Eyemouth born man who built and sailed the Cutty Sark. At once we became friends. Mr Reid and family saw me onboard a steamer bound to Victoria and Seattle and then I went by train to Portland and thence to San Francisco.

It was there that I experienced the only mishap during my long journey to and from southern California.

I had been seeing the sights in San Francisco and found out the time for the train to Los Angeles. I wired my friends in Long Beach saying that I would be leaving on the two-thirty train and I would be with them on the first train in the morning. Then, seated in the waiting room, I wrote a few letters and used my pocket book for a writing desk . . . my stop-off return ticket being inside which I laid on the seat as I put stamps on each letter. I then left the railway station, crossed the street to the Post Office, posted the letters and then went for dinner at a café. Afterwards I went to the depot as it was nearly time for the train. It was then that I realised my pocket book with my railway ticket, which had cost me so much money was missing.

I returned to the Post Office and the postmaster questioned all of the staff, but no one had seen my ticket. I went where I ate dinner, but no better luck there. I then remembered I had left it on the seat in the waiting room, but by then it had gone. I reported the same to the station authority who, after some questioning, believed my word and gave it to me just in time to get my train.

I arrived at seven thirty the next morning at Long Beach. I had many conversations with nice intelligent folk during my long train journey. The days never seemed long; so many passengers came to talk with me. I stayed a few weeks at Long Beach and visited Pasadena and many other places. I was invited by a medical doctor of the U.S. Navy to stay a week with him at San Diego.

The Methodist Church at Long Beach sent me as their delegate to Los Angeles to the Great World Sunday-School Convention which proved a rare treat to me. I shall never forget these great gatherings of eight thousand people at each meeting in that monster building. There were twenty-five thousand folk at one open air meeting. Strange to say while forging through that great company I made acquaintance with some folk from Aberdeen.

I returned to Toledo by the southern route and went to Grand Canyon – a five hundred and seventy-four mile run, but enjoyed the wonderful scenery there. I crossed the desert of Arizona, visited New Mexico, Kansas City, Colorado and many other cities on my way east to Toledo. I then had quite an exciting time searching for my son Jamie's certificate of his birth, and was informed that the office was burned to the ground and all papers were destroyed. That was very awkward, as my son was anxious to make his name in California. I went to see the judge at the Probate Court and was told that I must find two witnesses of very good standing who must take the oath that my son Jamie was born at Toledo, U.S.A. And Mr Craig and Mr Fred La France, my oldest chums, kindly wrote out affidavits and took the oath regarding my son's birth and the Probate Court gave me a citizenship certificate.

I hurried to New York and sailed on board the *SS Caledonia* and while on that voyage to Glasgow the Captain invited me on to the bridge and treated me very kindly, which helped to make the long journey over sea and land a real treat.

After I arrived in Bonnie Scotland I had to visit many folks in different towns in order to keep my promise to so many of their friends in so many different parts of Canada and in America who had begged me to call on their friends when I arrived home.

No one can understand the grandeur of meeting friends in a foreign land who have been away for many years unless they go through the same experience. They have so many questions to ask and so many stories to listen to regarding the days of yore. Then the traveller must say

'*Fare you well*', which gives us pain. Yet the kindly feeling and friendly tears filled our souls so that words refused to come. And as I turned the bend of the road I felt a lump in my throat when we waived to each other, which may be the last time we shall meet on earth.

But I will always cherish happy memories of meeting and parting with '*sae many of our ain folk sae far frae hame.*' One must go through that experience in order to understand it.

I am now resting on my oars, but find it hard to believe I am old and when I see the steamers passing by our harbour I have a yearning to start again. And I could have a modern steamer at short notice.

But I have enough money to keep me clear of the Poor House unless something happens that I don't know anything about.

James Lough
Master Mariner
17 George Street
Eyemouth

POSTSCRIPT

James Lough, truly the Noblest Work of God, lived on for a further
eleven years after he sent his memoirs off to America in 1929. Illness
eventually took its toll, and following two strokes James died at the age of
eighty-three, poignantly, on October 14 1940, the fifty-ninth anniversary
of the Eyemouth Fishing Disaster.

John Craig and Annie Losee never left Ohio. Though John went into
semi-retirement when he sold off the Toledo shipyard and his sons left
for Long Beach in 1907/8, Mr Craig continued as a shrewd and well
respected businessman. He was a director of the First National Bank and
President or Vice-President of a clutch of Toledo companies. During the
Great War he worked as an assistant to the director of the Wood Ship
Department of the Naval Offices and later did much to encourage the
establishment of industry in Toledo. As with James Lough, family was
all-important to John and Annie Craig and the presentation by their
granddaughter Ruth Craig Merrill of 'Episodes of My Life' on their
sixty-seventh wedding anniversary must have been a wonderful party.

Annie Losee Craig died on 10 November 1932. Her beloved husband,
Captain John Craig, died on 14 January 1934. Both are buried in Toledo.

BIRLINN LTD (incorporating John Donald and Polygon) is
one of Scotland's leading publishers with over four hundred
titles in print. Should you wish to be put on our catalogue
mailing list **contact**:

Catalogue Request
Birlinn Ltd
West Newington House
10 Newington Road
Edinburgh EH9 1QS
Scotland, UK

Tel: + 44 (0) 131 668 4371
Fax: + 44 (0) 131 668 4466
e-mail: info@birlinn.co.uk

Postage and packing is free within the UK. For overseas
orders, postage and packing (airmail) will be charged at
30% of the total order value.

For more information, or to order online, visit our website at
www.birlinn.co.uk

Birlinn